SMALL CONGREGATION, BIG POTENTIAL

Small Congregation, Big Potential

Ministry in the Small Membership Church

LYLE E. SCHALLER

Abingdon Press

Nashville

SMALL CONGREGATION, BIG POTENTIAL
MINISTRY IN THE SMALL MEMBERSHIP CHURCH

Copyright © 2003 by Abingdon Press

All rights reserved.

This book is printed on acid-free paper.

Library of Congress Cataloging-in-Publication Data

Schaller, Lyle E.
  Small congregation, big potential : ministry in the small membership church / Lyle E. Schaller.
    p. cm.
  ISBN 0-687-03656-9 (alk. paper)
  1. Small churches—United States.   2. Pastoral theology—United States.
3. Protestant churches—United States.   I. Title.
  BV637.8.S32   2003
  253—dc22   2003017291

Unless otherwise noted, Scripture quotations are from the *New Revised Standard Version of the Bible*, copyright 1989, by the Division of Christian Education of the National Council of the Churches of Christ in the United States of America. Used by permission.

Those marked RSV are taken from the *Revised Standard Version of the Bible*, copyright 1946, 1952, 1971 by the Division of Christian Education of the National Council of the Churches of Christ in the United States of America. Used by permission. All rights reserved.

03 04 05 06 07 08 09 10 11 12—10 9 8 7 6 5 4 3 2 1

MANUFACTURED IN THE UNITED STATES OF AMERICA

To
John and Connie Usry

CONTENTS

INTRODUCTION

The best-known small Christian church in the United States undoubtedly is the Little Brown Church in the Vale, located at 2730 Cheyenne Avenue, three miles northeast of Nashua, Iowa. It was made famous by the song composed in the middle of the 19th century by William S. Pitts that opens with the line, "There's a church in the valley by the wildwood, no lovelier spot in the dale." The words were written long before a church was constructed on that site. The current meeting place was constructed during the Civil War. It was closed for renovation for several years back at the end of the 19th century but has housed a continuing worshiping community for the past 90 years.

That paragraph includes one major error! The congregation housed in that building is *not* a small church! With a current membership slightly over 100 and averaging about 60 at worship, it ranks near the bottom of the middle third in size among all congregations in American Protestantism. Like most midsized American Protestant congregations, it carries a denominational affiliation—in this case with the United Church of Christ.

The Little Brown Church in the Vale also displays a few other characteristics that suggest it is not a typical small American Protestant congregation. First, it welcomes thousands of visitors every year. Second, the current pastor attempts to limit the number of weddings to a maximum of 12 in any one day, but that ceiling has been raised on several occasions. Third, the number of weddings in recent years has dropped to only 400 to 500 annually. The annual average for the 1914–2000 era was close to 900! Fourth, it is served by a resident pastor who is half of a clergy couple—a pattern that is increasingly common, but not the norm. Fifth, the current resident pastor is a woman. That is an increasingly common pattern for small and midsized Protestant and Roman Catholic congregations in America, but not yet the norm.

Sixth, like a growing number of small and midsized American Protestant congregations, it does not depend entirely on the offerings of current members to pay the bills. Many others rely on income from investments and/or memorials. The Little Brown Church uses fees for services to help cover expenses.

Seventh, unlike the majority of small and midsized American Protestant congregations, the Little Brown Church enjoys the advantages of a long-tenured minister. The current pastor began her ministry with this congregation in March 1994 with her husband as a clergy team, and became the solo pastor in January 2002.

Eighth, unlike most small and midsized Protestant congregations, the Little Brown Church attracts a huge crowd for its annual reunion the first weekend in August. Tens of thousands of American Protestant churches schedule their big crowd of the year for Easter Sunday—and are delighted when the attendance is double or triple the annual average worship attendance. The Little Brown Church schedules their big Sunday for the middle of the "summer slump," and the attendance is 7 to 10 times the average Sunday morning attendance for the whole year!

Ninth, the Little Brown Church enjoys an international constituency. Visitors come from Japan, Germany, Mexico, and dozens of other countries year after year.

Tenth, the Little Brown Church maintains an exceptionally attractive and informative website (www.littlebrownchurch.org). Finally, the Little Brown Church in rural Iowa illustrates a central theme of this book. That catch-all category, "the small American Protestant church," is about as useful as such categories as "teenagers," "women," "blacks," "professors," "criminals," "men," "Muslims," "lawyers," or "farmers." The common thread linking all those categories is in each one no two are alike. Each one differs from all the others in that category.

The responsibilities of the Reverend Linda Myren as the pastor of the Little Brown Church in the Vale differ greatly from the responsibilities of her husband, Bob, who currently is the pastor of a similar sized United Church of Christ congregation in rural Iowa, but that also is true of every other minister serving a small Protestant congregation in the United States in the 21st century.

At this point it is necessary to draw a line between two definitions of the term "small membership church." The "popular" definition is the congregation that is too small to both (a) own and maintain its own set-apart-for-church-use-only meeting place and (b) attract and retain the services of a full-time and fully credentialed resident pastor. Thus tens of thousands of small American Protestant congregations (a) meet in rented facilities or in private homes or storefronts, or share facilities with another congregation and/or (b) are served by a pastor who concurrently serves one or more other congregations, or by a lay minister or a bivocational minister or a retired pastor. This definition includes the vast majority of all American Protestant congregations averaging 125 or fewer at worship, but there are many exceptions. The Little Brown Church is one exception. The statistical definition divides the estimated 325,000 American Protestant congregations, exclusive of small house churches, into three categories: small, midsized, and large. The one-third that average 55 or fewer at worship can be classified as small. The one-third that average between 56 and 115 at worship can be labeled midsized, and those averaging more than 115 at worship can be placed in the large-church category. This definition explains why the Little Brown Church in rural Iowa belongs in the midsized group.

With a few exceptions, however, the contents of this book use that popular definition. Chapter 12 is one exception. It has been written for the leaders in congregations at the large end of this statistical definition of the midsized congregations and also stretched to include those "large churches" averaging 115 to 125 at worship. (See chapters 1 and 2 for an elaboration of this classification system.)

If one-half of all American Protestant congregations average fewer than 75 at worship, why are there so few really big congregations and so many small ones? That is the subject of chapter 3, but the central point is that the "natural" size for a congregation in American Protestantism is an average worship attendance of somewhere between 18 and 40. That is the beginning point for anyone seeking to design a customized ministry plan for a particular small church.

A Dozen Assumptions

Like every other book written on the state of the church in contemporary American Protestantism, this one is based on a series of assumptions. It may help the reader if a dozen of these are identified here. The first is most Americans no longer live in a culture organized around a scarcity of resources. We now live in a culture overflowing with a huge variety of resources. One of these is an abundance of gifted, skilled, deeply committed, and creative Christian laypersons who are waiting to be challenged. That is the basic assumption underlying chapter 6.

A parallel depository of unprecedented resources can be found in larger congregations that are able and willing, if invited, to share their abundance with smaller churches. That assumption is central to both chapters 6 and 7.

One consequence, in this contemporary American ecclesiastical economy of abundance, is the vast majority of small congregations in American Protestantism are not limited to only four or five options as they plan for ministry in the 21st century. They have dozens of options. Thus this book is designed for leaders who are not handicapped by only five fingers on each hand, but who own gloves with 15 or 20 fingers for each hand. They do not have to remove their shoes and socks to count their options.

A persuasive argument could be made that the crucial line of demarcation separating one group of policymakers from another is this issue. Those responsible for most of the decisions influencing the future of the small Protestant congregation tend to plan on the basis of a shortage of resources. By contrast the decision-makers in the large and numerically growing churches tend to assume an abundance of resources. Each group creates a self-fulfilling prophecy.

The second assumption is a theme repeated throughout this book. The natural, normal, and comfortable size for a worshiping community in American Protestantism includes somewhere between 18 and 40 worshipers at the typical weekend worship service. While it is true that an uncounted and growing number of lay-led house churches plus at least 6,000 organized churches are smaller, that 18-to-40-size bracket appears to be the norm. One alternative is to accept and affirm that as the norm. Another is to conceptualize a congregation as a collection of worshiping communities of various sizes plus cells, choirs, circles, classes, committees, fellowships, groups, missional teams, organizations, and task forces where individuals can acquire a sense of belonging despite the anonymity that comes with size. A different approach is to organize the congregation around the creativity, personality, gifts, organizational skills, priorities, and goals of a magnetic leader who will lead that congregation until the second coming of Christ.

The crucial point here is that small Protestant church averaging two to three dozen people at worship should be affirmed as a legitimate order of God's creation.

The third assumption is the vast majority of congregations in American Protestantism are not organized to welcome a flood of newcomers. To challenge them to grow overlooks that point. Long-term substantial numerical growth would require them to abandon their current central organizing principles and culture and replace them with a new set of organizing principles and a new culture. This is discussed in greater detail in chapters 3 and 11. Those differences in central organizing principles also are far more influential than denominational affiliation or location or date of organization in distinguishing between the very large and the very small congregations in American Protestantism.

A fourth assumption is that the possibility of merger with another small congregation should rank no higher than 28 on that list of 25 options open to contemporary small American congregations as they plan for their ministry in the 21st century. (See chapter 13.)

Should dissolution be on that list? YES! Although that course of action is not discussed elsewhere in this book, it belongs on that list of options for three reasons. First, an average of at least 1,500 American Protestant congregations choose that option every year. That means it is widely perceived as a realistic alternative. Second, in more than a few cases an interventionist recommends it. Third, and most important, the Christian gospel is a message filled with hope, a belief in the Resurrection, and a conviction that God is alive and at work in his world. When the members of any Christian worshiping community, regardless of size, do not share any hope for the future, it may be prudent to dissolve. It is difficult to proclaim a meaningful and persuasive message of God's love, grace, and redemption in an absence of hope and joy. This pilgrim has zero competence to offer constructive advice on how to proclaim the Christian gospel in an institutional environment in which hope is completely absent.

The fifth assumption is the combination of modern technology and affluence poses the greatest threat to the future of tens of thousands of small American Protestant churches. The automobile has made obsolete the conviction that every congregation should serve a constituency living within a mile or two or three of the meeting place. Television has elevated people's expectations of what they have a right to expect from church. Television has revolutionized the definition of "good preaching." Affluence and the Internet have convinced most Americans they have not only a right, but also a moral obligation to "shop for the best buys" in motor vehicles, housing, clothes, schools, food, entertainment, health care, legal counsel, financial services, recreation, and church.

In other words, today's Christian congregations serve in a far more competitive culture than was true in 1925 or 1975.

The sixth assumption is that affluence and modern technology have greatly expanded the list of options open to the vast majority of small American Protestant congregations from three or four to at least two dozen. That is a central theme of chapters 4 through 12, and 14.

The videotape now enables members of the congregation averaging 18 at worship to enjoy all the advantages of the small congregation and also be nurtured by the very best of contemporary preaching—and at a bargain cost!

A seventh assumption is that one characteristic of the contemporary American economy is that it has been creating concentrations in the marketplace. An expanding proportion of food and fiber is being produced by a shrinking number of farms. A half dozen national corporations sell a growing proportion of the groceries. A diminishing number of banks hold a growing proportion of bank deposits. A shrinking number of public high schools account for a growing proportion of the students. In 1986 the top 5 percent of personal income taxpayers in the United States, as measured by their adjusted gross income, paid 42 percent of the personal income taxes received by the United States government. In 1999 the top 5 percent paid 56 percent of those dollars. A decreasing number of corporations account for a growing proportion of the daily newspapers in America. Approximately 30 percent of the Protestant churches in America account for 70 percent of the worshipers on the typical weekend.

Overlapping that is an eighth assumption. The differences among motor vehicles, houses, universities, retail stores, major league baseball teams, farms, shoes, aircraft, restaurants, physicians, elementary schools, churches, and people are greater than ever before in American history. One consequence is the role or business plans or goals rarely have a complete overlap. One size will not fit everyone. That also means each congregation should design its own customized ministry plan as the leaders look ahead to ministry in the 21st century. An action plan that is appropriate for one congregation probably will not fit ninety-nine others in the same regional judicatory.

When that trend is combined with the increasingly dominant role of big institutions, that often means a retailer, a farmer, a physician, a motel chain, a grocery store, a law office, or a church will be well advised to match its assets with a precisely defined niche in this highly competitive marketplace. That is the theme of chapter 8.

A ninth assumption is that the recent trend toward one enterprise serving constituents at several geographically separate locations will accelerate. Today one farmer may work the land at three or four locations. A medical clinic may serve patients at five geographically separate centers. A bank may have branches in a dozen supermarkets. A real estate firm may have five local offices. The local public library may operate at four different locations. One congregation may operate under one name with one message, one governing board, one staff, and one treasury, and may gather people for the corporate worship of God at seven locations. This trend opens the door to a variety of new scenarios and is a theme of chapters 6 through 9, and 12.

The tenth assumption is the theme of chapter 5. The problem is not a shortage of talented ministers. The apparent shortage of talent is really a consequence of ecclesiastical systems that set ministers up to fail rather than to create an ecological environment that fosters success.

Eleventh, a crucial assumption is the American culture is increasingly organized around the value of long-term relationships. One example is the growing number of state governments that have concluded they cannot afford the economic and social costs of divorce. A second is the increasing number of public schools that are offering financial rewards to teachers for long tenure. While no one can prove causation, the correlation between numerical growth and long pastorates suggests that any small Protestant congregation hoping for substantial numerical growth in the years ahead will be well advised to attract a pastor who is a highly skilled agent of planned change, a persuasive communicator of the orthodox Christian faith, and who also expects this to be a 20- or 30-year relationship, not a brief transition between two other assignments.

Finally, the last of these 12 assumptions may be the recipient of the largest number of dissenters. The guiding assumption is the traditional denominational systems in American Protestantism have two choices. One is to change and be responsive to the demands of a new ecclesiastical landscape. One scenario is to shift from geographically defined regional judicatories to encouraging the creation of new affinity-based judicatories.[1] A second example is to look for new sources of money in this increasingly competitive scramble for the charitable dollar.[2] A third set of scenarios is the focus of chapter 16.

The alternative is for these traditional denominational systems to be written off as obsolete or irrelevant or, worst of all, as unneeded adversaries.

Is This Book for You?

It is impossible for a sinful human being to write a book that addresses the agenda of every potential reader. At least 10 groups of American Protestant leaders should not waste their time reading this book. (It is completely acceptable, however, for them to purchase it as a gift to a friend.)

1. If you are completely satisfied with the status quo in your congregation and/or your denomination, this book is not for you. If your dream is to perpetuate the status quo for another decade or two, this book will be of little help.

2. If you are absolutely convinced the second coming of Christ is only a few weeks away, you should not waste time reading this book. You have more urgent and important responsibilities on your agenda.

3. If you believe your denomination should increase the number of small congregations, this book is not for you. That trend

may be well underway now. If you do want to accelerate it, limit pastoral tenure to five years. Another half dozen suggestions can be found in the last few pages of chapter 13. If the goal is to plant a new mission that plateaus in size with an average worship attendance of fewer than 100, a dozen keys to that strategy can be found in chapter 3. If that is your primary agenda, however, don't buy this book, borrow a copy for a few days.

4. If you are convinced that the most effective way to create strength is to merge weakness with weakness and that therefore mergers are the best alternative for most small churches, this book is not for you. That chapter on mergers will not reinforce your convictions.

5. Perhaps most important, if you are convinced that next year will closely resemble 1955 and congregational leaders in American Protestantism should design their ministries after the 1955 models, this book is not for you.

6. If you are convinced that on at least 45 weekends out of every year the sermon in every church should be delivered in person—by a resident pastor, preferably one who has earned a degree from an accredited seminary, and who knows most or all the worshipers in that gathered community—this may not be the book for you.

7. If you are convinced the norm for a congregation in contemporary American Protestantism is one that averages at least 100 people at worship, is served by a full-time pastor, and also owns and maintains its own meeting place, this book may not be for you.

8. If you believe that evangelizing the unchurched should be a central purpose of every Christian congregation in America, this book will not reinforce your convictions on that point.

9. If you agree that a resident pastor cannot be expected to articulate every facet of the Christian gospel to that gathered community, and therefore it is beneficial to the worshipers to welcome a new minister every three or four or five years, this clearly is not the book for you.

10. If you share the conviction that every Christian congregation in America should be prepared to welcome and respond

effectively to the personal and spiritual needs of everyone, regardless of age, gender, marital status, nationality, race, sexual orientation, theological stance, occupation, language, or income, this clearly is not the book for you.

Those disclaimers are required by this new consumer-driven American culture. That is but one of many reasons why the context for ministry for the small-member church differs so greatly from when this writer was the pastor of three small congregations back in the 1950s.

CHAPTER ONE

HOW DO YOU DEFINE SMALL?

Jesus declared, "For where two or three are gathered in my name, there am I in the midst of them" (Matthew 18:20 RSV). While I am reluctant to quarrel with Scripture, for simple pragmatic reasons, the definition of the small church in this book begins with a larger number. This was decided in spite of the fact that in reporting their worship attendance, scores of American Protestant congregations report an average of one to three. In 1999, for example, seven United Methodist congregations reported an average worship attendance of one, while 22 others reported two as their average worship attendance. (Ten of these 29 churches reported a membership of zero to five.)

For this discussion, however, the operational definition of small begins with congregations reporting a worship attendance of three, four, or five, rather than one or two. In the year 2000, that included 25 Assemblies of God congregations, 49 Episcopal parishes, 40 Southern Baptist churches, 32 PCUSA, 208 United Methodist churches, 8 Disciples of Christ congregations, 5 ELCA parishes, and 3 Presbyterian Church of America congregations.

At the other end of this size spectrum, the largest congregations to be included in this discussion are those averaging 101 to 125 at worship. That is a broad category and includes approximately 25,000 or about the same number that average more than 350 at worship. Every autumn, Southern Baptist churches are asked to report their worship attendance for the last Sunday in September. The reports for 2000 included 2,726 congregations reporting a worship attendance of 101 to 125. That compares with 2,529 that reported an attendance of 51 to 60 (a far narrower size bracket), and the 1,004 congregations reporting an attendance of exactly 40 at Sunday morning worship. (See appendix A for reports from other denominations.)

In other words, the definition of "small church" in this book includes those congregations averaging 125 or fewer at the principal weekend worship service.

How Many Does That Include?

In most of the larger American Protestant denominations that definition includes a thousand or more congregations. (The vast majority of American Protestant denominations, associations, fellowships, and movements include fewer than 1,000 congregations.) Approximately two-thirds of the affiliated congregations report an average worship attendance of 125 or fewer. In those traditions in which the

Proportion of Congregations Averaging 125 or Fewer at Worship	
Assemblies of God	71%
Baptist General Conference	60%
Disciples of Christ*	71%
Episcopal Church USA	69%
Evangelical Free Church	56%
Presbyterian Church in America	62%
Presbyterian Church (USA)	70%
Southern Baptist Convention	69%
United Church of Christ*	70%
United Methodist Church	78%

*A large number of congregations did not report worship attendance.

24

operational policies encourage the emergence of larger congregations, that proportion is smaller; while in those in which the operational policies discourage the emergence of large congregations, the proportion of small churches naturally will be higher.

Our database indicates that out of the estimated 325,000 organized Protestant churches in the United States at the end of 2000, approximately 165,000 averaged 75 or fewer at worship and another 60,000 averaged between 76 and 125 at worship.

Why Choose 125?

Many readers may prefer to define small American Protestant congregations as those averaging 100 or fewer at worship. That is a good round number and easy to defend. One reason to use it is that relatively few congregations averaging less than 100 at worship are served by a full-time and fully credentialed resident pastor, but a substantial number in the 100-125 bracket do enjoy that advantage. One reason to lower that end of the definition to 99 or 100 average worship attendance is a congregation averaging 110 at worship will utilize a different set of criteria in the self-evaluation process than will the very small church averaging 15, 18, or 20 at worship.

One reason to use 125 rather than 100 in this definition is the growing agreement that an average worship attendance of 125 or more is the contemporary minimum to be able to economically afford, to justify in terms of the workload, and to attract, challenge, and retain a full-time and fully credentialed resident pastor.

A better reason is a worship attendance of approximately 125 usually is required to be able to mobilize the resources required to meet the expectations that younger generations bring to church. (See chapter 4.) The expectations people project of a church in the early years of the 21st century are far greater than they were in the 1950s. One consequence is more resources are required to meet those expectations.

Another reason is illustrated by ninth-graders. Where should ninth-graders go to school? They are clearly too big and too mature to be mixed in with seventh- and eighth-graders. They also are too young and too immature to be in the same school with eleventh- and twelfth-graders. (See chapter 12.) The parallel is, where in the classification system do we place these congregations averaging 101 to 125 at worship? One answer is to stop debating the question, assign a separate chapter to them, and move on to another subject.

The 20th-century Context

The last truly comprehensive census of religious congregations in the United States was conducted by the United States Bureau of the Census in 1906. The bureau also conducted a census of religious bodies for 1916, 1926, and 1936, but none of these were as comprehensive as that benchmark survey of 1906 that was published in 1910.[1]

That 1906 census collected data on 212,230 religious congregations, up from the 165,151 counted in 1890. That 1906 total included 195,618 Protestant churches, plus 12,482 Roman Catholic parishes, and 1,709 Jewish congregations. That total of 195,618 represented a 27.8 percent increase from the 153,054 Protestant total of 1890.

How many Christian churches are in the United States today? No one knows. Back in 1906 it was easier to answer that question. The Bureau of the Census relies on reports from 186 religious bodies for nearly all of their data. That census of 1906 counted 1,079 independent or nondenominational Protestant congregations, up from the 155 counted in 1890.

The most comprehensive recent census used data for the year 2000 and was conducted by the Glenmary Research Center. They collected data from 149 religious bodies that together included 268,254 congregations, including 21,791 Catholic parishes, 3,727 Jewish congregations, and 1,705 independent churches. It is worth noting that 55 of the 149 reporting religious bodies include fewer than 100 congregations.[2]

Back in the nineteenth century the vast majority of Christian congregations in America were affiliated with a religious body such as Roman Catholic, Eastern Orthodox, Baptist, or Lutheran. One part of the explanation for that pattern was most congregations traced their religious heritage back to western Europe, where denominational affiliations were the norm. A second reason was most of the American Protestant denominations specialized in serving congregations. These services included enlisting and sending Christian missionaries to other parts of the world, providing materials produced by the denominational publishing house, screening and approving candidates for ordination, planting new missions, administering charitable and institutions such as homes, orphanages, and schools, and offering leadership training events.

A third influential force, which has been largely neglected by most church historians, was the railroads. Clergymen were entitled to request a pass or a discount on their railroad passenger ticket. One required qualification was that clergyperson had to be listed on the roster of ordained ministers in the current yearbook for that denomination. No listing meant no clergy pass!

A fourth factor was that network of intradenominational ministerial fellowships. In many denominations they were the gatekeepers to ordination. That denominational affiliation was an important component of a pastor's professional identity. One common consequence was the congregation seeking a pastor chose their favorite candidate. That candidate, however, required this: "If I accept your invitation to become your new pastor, your congregation must agree to join my denomination." Local church histories covering the nineteenth century describe that arrangement. In some cases that meant the congregation switched its denominational affiliation. In others it meant what had been an independent church now carried a denominational affiliation.

The twentieth century brought the creation of thousands of nondenominational Protestant churches in America. Others seceded from their denomination to become independent. More recently the flood of immigrants from the Pacific Rim and

Latin America, plus the emergence of thousands of nondenominational congregations created to serve American-born, Caribbean-born, or African-born blacks have combined to increase the number and variety of independent Protestant congregations in America.

The 1960s fed the fires of anti-institutionalism and affirmed the right of individual autonomy. One result is the number of independent Protestant congregations in America has increased at an accelerated pace during the past four decades.

How many Christian congregations are in the United States today? No one knows. Back in 1906 a reasonably accurate count could be derived from an examination of denominational reports. Today those reports tell only part of the story. A reasonable guess is that in 1906 the actual number of independent Protestant churches probably was closer to 2,000 than to the 1,079 reported by that special census. Today that number is probably closer to 50,000, plus an estimated additional 25,000 nondenominational house churches.[3]

This book is based on the assumption that at least 325,000 organized Protestant congregations exist in America today. That represents a 67 percent increase between 1906 and 2000. The population of the United States increased three and a half times during those 94 years.

That total of 325,000 Protestant churches includes all of the ethnic minority and immigrant congregations, but it does not include that uncounted but clearly growing number of lay-led house churches that resemble voluntary fellowships rather than organized churches.

Our database includes worship attendance figures for approximately 160,000 American Protestant congregations. We know that our database greatly underrepresents (1) congregations consisting largely of American-born blacks, (2) immigrant churches, (3) nondenominational or independent churches, and (4) congregations that were born but disappeared within a few years following their birth.

What must be defined as an informed estimate is that approximately 70 percent of those 325,000 Protestant congregations average 125 or fewer at weekend worship. That comes out to approximately 225,000 congregations.

Seven Categories

For this and other discussions we have divided those 325,000 American Protestant congregations into seven categories. The largest group includes an estimated 50,000 congregations that average 25 or fewer at worship. These can be described as fellowships. Approximately 1 out of 6 or 7 American Protestant churches falls into this category.

The next category consists of what we are describing as the norm. The normal and natural size for a worshiping community in American Protestantism is 18 to 40 at worship. (See chapter 3.) We have redefined it here to include all congregations averaging 26 to 50 at worship. That total of 40,000 congregations represents 1 out of 8 Protestant churches in America.

Our largest, and the most inclusive category, includes the estimated 110,000 congregations averaging 51 to 100 at worship. That includes 1 out of 3 Protestant congregations in America.

Our fourth category includes those organized Protestant churches averaging 101 to 125 at worship. That number is estimated to be 25,000, or 1 of 13.

A fifth and extremely broad category includes the estimated 75,000 "midsized" churches averaging between 126 and 350 at worship. A sixth category consists of the 18,000 "large" churches averaging 351 to 800 at worship while the smallest group plays by a different "rulebook." These are the 7,000 congregations averaging more than 800 at worship and are the focus of other resources.[4]

An Interesting Question

The use of average worship attendance as a criterion for describing American Protestant congregations did not begin to be widely used until the 1950s, and most denominations did not include that question in their data banks until the 1960s or later. Therefore we do not have a long historical record in the use of this yardstick. By contrast, thousands of congregations and several denominations do have year-by-year reports on average Sunday school attendance going back to the 1920s or earlier.

An old adage among professionals in the field of evaluation declares, "You count what you believe is important and whatever you count becomes important." Does this recent recognition of the value of counting and reporting the attendance when people gather for the corporate worship of God suggest that in a growing number of religious groups in America worship is now as important as the Sunday school in reviewing congregational life? Or, is this simply a belated recognition that average worship attendance is a more reliable, a more realistic, and a more sensitive yardstick for measuring size than either membership, or financial receipts, or the number of dollars sent to some other religious organization?

One of the consequences of this recent expression in the number of congregations reporting their worship attendance is the emergence of four trends. One is the recent sharp increase in the number of very large congregations reporting an average worship attendance of more than 800. A second is the growing proportion of younger American Protestant churchgoers who choose a very large church. The third is that shrinking number of midsized Protestant churches in the United States. The fourth is the recent increase in the number averaging fewer than 75 at worship. This fourth trend motivated the writing of this book. Together these four trends also introduce the next chapter.

CHAPTER TWO

THAT'S NOT A CATEGORY!

One of the central ways we make sense of experience is by making differences. The world presents itself without inherent order, and our impulse is to place things in piles, count them, and name them.

—Lee S. Shulman[1]

A persuasive argument could be made that one of the most misleading efforts would be to offer a two-day workshop or write a book for leaders in small Protestant congregations. That could be the equivalent of focusing on a category such as "immigrants" or "teenagers" or "men" or "Americans born in the 1970–1982 era" or "women" or "American-born blacks" or "retirees" or "Asians" or "Euro-Americans." Each one is an extremely broad category. Each one includes millions of people. Each one consists of subgroups in which the differences between the subgroups exceed the similarities within that large category.

For example, that age cohort born in the 1970–1992 era includes record numbers of (1) people currently in jail or prison, (2) female college graduates, (3) physically disabled adults, (4) never-married mothers, (5) millionaires, and (6) Americans of Asian ancestry. The cultural differences are far more significant than age as a point of commonality.

31

Likewise, "small church" really is not a homogeneous category. That new Lutheran mission that held its first public worship service four months ago and currently is averaging 60 at Sunday morning worship is a small church. In 2001, 72 percent of all ELCA parishes were averaging more than 60 at worship. A United Church of Christ congregation founded in 1890 in a small rural community in Ohio that averaged 60 at worship last year—up from 53 10 years ago, but down from its peak of 84 in 1958—also is a small church. The two, however, have little in common. The first is driven by a future orientation. The second is driven by 11 decades of local traditions.

Similarly, that nine-year-old Korean-American congregation in California serves a constituency in which most of the adult males were born in Korea, have earned at least two academic degrees, and enjoy an annual income of more than $60,000. It averages 45 at worship but has little in common with that working-class Haitian congregation in Florida that also averages 45 at worship.

How Many Categories?

If, for discussion purposes, we focus on the estimated 200,000 congregations in American Protestantism that average 100 or fewer at worship, we end up with more than 10 million separate categories after identifying only a dozen primary lines of demarcation.

The first line of demarcation could be the skin color of the majority of the constituents (white, black, brown, yellow, and multicultural). The second is more complicated and divides each of those first five categories by language, ancestry, place (nation) of birth, and place of parents' birth. Multiplying those first five categories of skin color by at least 80 cuts in this second round brings us to 400 categories. Multiply that by only five categories for geographical location of the meeting place (center city, old suburban, new suburban, exurban, and rural), and the table now contains 2,000 cells after only three cuts. Add a fourth round consisting of only three divisions for the dominant age cohort among the adult constituents (born before 1941, born 1941–1960, born 1961–1985), and we have 6,000 cells in the table. Multiply that by four divisions for social-economic-educational class, and we have 24,000 categories. Multiply that by four broad categories for theology (fundamentalist, evangelical, middle-of-the-road, and liberal), and we now have 96,000 cells in the table labeled "Small American Protestant Churches."

We could slice it by the marital status of the majority of the constituents and/or average worship attendance and/or ownership versus rental or lease of the place of worship and/or the annual operating expenditures and/or by the length of the time that congregation has been meeting at the same address and/or at least five divisions for the current choice in regard to ministerial leadership. If we used all 12 of those lines of demarcation, we could end up with 135 million cells in that chart designed to recognize the differences among these 200,000 small churches, and we still have not accounted for differences in the influence of denominational affiliation (controlling, moderate, or none) or in the system followed in congregational decision making. The result would be approximately 99 percent of the cells in that table would be empty, and most of the remaining 1 percent would include only one or two small churches.

The point of that brief exercise in arithmetic is fourfold. The first is to affirm the validity of that frequently heard comment, "But our church is different!" The typical small American Protestant congregation may have a twin in that table described here, but it is highly unlikely it is one of a set of quintuplets.

Second, without going beyond a dozen lines of demarcation in classifying churches, this explains why offering four or five options to small congregations usually will produce the response, "None of those fit us."

Third, and a central theme of this book, is that table filled with at least 135 million cells explains why the ideal strategy calls for designing a customized ministry plan for every congregation, regardless of size.

Fourth, while it may not be the best criterion, size as measured by average worship attendance, is a relatively objective line of demarcation. It is easy to understand and also widely used. It also is a sensitive barometer for identifying changes in a congregation's capability to attract and retain constituents.

Who Is the Audience?

The intended audience for this book consists primarily of three groups of potential readers. The largest, by far, includes congregational leaders, both paid and volunteer, who are in one of those 225,000 American congregations averaging 125 or fewer at worship. That broad definition includes approximately 7 out of 10 Protestant congregations in the United States. That, however, is far from a homogeneous group. The simplest system we can use to translate that number 225,000 into comprehensible terms is, it includes approximately 90,000 congregations averaging 50 or fewer at worship, another 75,000 averaging 51 to 75 at worship, 35,000 averaging 76 to 100, and "only" 25,000 averaging 101 to 125 at worship. For comparison purposes an estimated 25,000 American Protestant churches average over 350 at worship.

A much smaller audience for this book consists of denominational policy makers (see chapters 16 and 17) and those professional staff members who act as advisors to congregational leaders.

The third potential audience includes seminary faculty and students, parish consultants, and others interested in the life and ministry of the small American Protestant congregation.

Where Do You Begin?

One useful beginning point in planning for ministry in the twenty-first century is to choose a planning model. One model calls for identifying strengths and assets and building on those strengths. A popular model calls for identifying problems and

devising solutions for those problems. In connectional denominations, one model calls for each congregation to begin by getting acquainted with the denominational strategy, goals, and
priorities for that particular regional judicatory and designing a
ministry plan that is consistent with that larger denominational
strategy. By contrast, the congregation that has just welcomed a
new pastor may begin by identifying the distinctive gifts, skills,
and priorities of that minister.

This traveler often begins with a medical analogy. The physician examines a patient and compares weight, pulse, blood pressure, blood count, and other characteristics with what is
considered normal for a patient of that age and gender, or with
similar measurements of that patient taken on a previous visit.

Three parallel questions for a congregational planning committee, a denominational staff person, or a parish consultant
could be (1) What is your average worship attendance? (2) Is that
up or down from a year ago? (3) What is normal for a church of
your type in your denomination? The next chapter describes
what is "normal." In American Protestantism as a whole, that is
an average worship attendance between 18 and 50 and usually
close to 35.

If it is below 18 or above 50, we ask, "How come?" In the congregation averaging 110 at worship, the answer may be, "We
really consist of seven overlapping congregations including two
adult Sunday school classes, our women's organization, an adult
choir, the teaching staff of the Sunday school, the volunteers on
the boards and committees that run this church, and a dozen people who are very close personal friends of our current pastor."

If the answer is 56, the explanation could be, "We were
launched to be a new mission four years ago with a guaranteed
five-year denominational subsidy. The design called for attracting
people who prefer the intimacy of a small church, so we've been
on a plateau in size for nearly two years."

If the answer is an average of 18 at worship, the explanation
may be, "This was founded to serve immigrants from Norway, but
the boats haven't been coming over recently."

A common response: "We now average 32 at worship, up from 31 four years ago. We have enough people to fill all the essential volunteer slots, we are able to pay our bills on time, we love one another, we care for anyone who is sick, we mourn the loss when someone dies, we enjoy the intimacy of our fellowship, and we appreciate the absence of complexity. Why are you bothering us?"

A highly productive planning model is based on systems theory and can be condensed to three introductory questions: (1) What do we believe God is calling this congregation to be and to be doing in the years ahead? In other words, what are the desired outcomes we believe God expects our congregation to produce? (2) If we conceptualize our congregation as a system, what are the outcomes this system is now producing? This question is based on the assumption that systems produce the outcomes they are designed to produce. (3) What changes must be made in our system in order to produce the desired outcomes? One example of the use of this planning model is described in those two rarely traveled roads in chapter 12.

A widely used planning model among the leaders of small American Protestant churches, as well as denominational officials, begins with the assumption there is a shortage of resources. Why do those small churches outnumber the midsized and large congregations by more than a 2-to-1 ratio? A common explanation is a shortage of resources such as money, leadership, real estate, creativity, seminary graduates who feel called to serve small congregations, or the absence of a firm commitment to evangelism.

This book is based on the assumption that only rarely is money the critical issue. The central "problem" is a product of several factors. The first is the natural, normal, and most comfortable size for a congregation in American Protestantism is represented by those averaging between 18 and 50 at worship. If a full-time and fully credentialed resident shepherd is perceived as essential, the most comfortable size is somewhere between 80 and 135 at worship.

The second influential factor is a growing proportion of American Protestant churchgoers bring expectations that can be fulfilled only by larger congregations that are able to mobilize the resources required to provide the relevance (a term with dozens of different operational definitions), quality, and choices that younger generations expect.

The third factor is change—which may or may not involve numerical growth—will be required for most of today's small churches to be able to reach, attract, serve, retain, assimilate, and challenge the generations born after 1965.

The fourth factor is that in the absence of a widely perceived crisis, the natural, normal, and predictable response to planned change initiated from within any organization is rejection. One contemporary example is the widespread resistance by professionals in the church to replacing the live preacher with a videotaped message.

A fifth variable is that inventory of gifted, skilled, deeply committed, and visionary lay volunteers is not uniformly distributed among the churches. Hundreds of congregations have a surplus, while tens of thousands are limited by a shortage. (See chapters 6 and 7.)

In other words, this is *not* a church-growth book. This book is based on the assumption that the most productive way to introduce change into any voluntary association is to offer realistic choices. It also is assumed that no one scenario will fit even a minority of any one of the many categories under that umbrella term "small church."

Therefore, rather than identify the current abundance of small churches as a "problem" or to attempt to place all of them in a single homogeneous category, it may be more productive to look briefly at why they are so numerous.

WHY SO MANY?

I n an economy increasingly dominated by big institutions (supermarkets, universities, corporate farms, medical clinics, discount stores, financial institutions, motor vehicle manufacturers, airlines, entertainment networks, and so forth), why do the majority of Protestant congregations in America report their average worship attendance is fewer than 75?

One response can be found by looking at the dynamics of groups.[1] If a study group is charged with the responsibility of researching and defining a new course of action for an organization, the optimum size is somewhere between 5 and 10 people, depending on how important it is to represent the views, values, and priorities of the various factors, interest groups, departments, and committees within that organization. The greater the value placed on a unanimous recommendation, the better a number close to five. From a worldwide perspective the most highly visible example is the permanent membership of the Security Council of the United Nations. Another example is in April 2000 only 5 percent of all American families included more than five persons, while 86 percent included two, three, or four persons. If the number of participants exceeds 9 or 10, the price of a unanimous recommendation usually requires significant compromises. The larger the size of that policy-making group, the greater the influence of the past and local traditions. One consequence is a disproportionately large number of very small Protestant congregations report an average worship attendance of eight.

If a high value is placed on performance and a willingness to make personal sacrifices in support of the group's goals or on behalf of fellow members of that group, the ideal size is about five or six, with 10 as the absolute maximum. This has been a central guiding principle for military organizations and for police officers and firefighters for centuries.

A second natural size for a group that places a high value on caring for one another, on sharing resources, on individual participation, on mutual support, and on intimacy is a maximum of 15 to 18 participants. This is often described as the maximum size for a seminar in graduate school, as the ideal size for a fifth-grade elementary school class, as the maximum size for a weekly adult Bible study and prayer group, and for certain military formations. It also is a common size for church choirs and for adult Sunday school classes.

It is no coincidence that a disproportionately large number of very small Protestant congregations report their average worship attendance is either 15 or 18.

Many years ago Lyndon B. Johnson was asked about life in the hill country of Texas where he had been reared. He replied that in the hill county the people cared for you when you were ill, and they mourned when you died. Add two phases—"they miss you when you're absent, and rejoice when you return"—and you have a summary of the culture of the small church.

Typically, it averages between 18 and 40 at worship. The longer the tenure of the current members and/or the stronger the kinship ties, the easier it is to average 35 to 40 at worship. That size also enables it to fill the essential volunteer positions and to mobilize the resources required to operate and maintain its own meeting place. In several American Protestant traditions, the four most frequently cited numbers when congregations report their worship attendance are 35, 30, 25, and 40—in that order.

Typically two to five times as many congregations will report a worship attendance of 35 as report a number over 1,000. (In the SBC in 2000 that ratio was 791 to 425, in the PCUSA it was 233 to 48, in the Assemblies of God 299 to 130, in the Episcopal Church USA 65 to 17, in the UMC in 1999 842 to 130, and in the ELCA 133 to 44. See appendix A.)

When the number of participants in a group exceeds 35 to 40, anonymity and complexity begin to undermine group cohesion. Major league baseball teams, elementary school classes, military organizations, church choirs, the traditional one-room country school, the number of beds on one floor of a wing of a hospital, neighborhood associations, and the number of residents on one floor of a college dormitory are among the many examples of how "the rule of forty" is reflected across American life. When the number of people exceeds forty, it is easy for the participants not to notice one or two absentees.

Another Perspective

For several decades social anthropologists have been studying the history of human settlements. One of their conclusions is that for most of the history of human beings on this planet, the typical human settlement included between 75 and 225 people of all ages. When that number reached 300, there was a tendency for some of the people to decide to leave and create a new community at another location. Once again anonymity and complexity combined to undermine group cohesion and the willingness to sacrifice on behalf of others. One contemporary illustration of that tendency is approximately one-half of those Protestant congregations that practice infant baptism report fewer than 200 baptized members, while well over one-half of those that use confirmation as the line of demarcation in counting members report fewer than 200 members. Those two patterns can be seen in Protestant missions on other continents as well as in most of the larger Protestant denominations in the United States.

On the local government scene in the U.S., the total number of legally incorporated villages and townships, each with a population under 250, exceeds the number of cities by a 3-to-1 ratio.

Who Are the Replacements?

Why do a majority of American Protestant congregations average fewer than 75 at worship? One part of the explanation is the nature of human relationships. Another factor, which is discussed in more detail in the next chapter, is that every year scores of what once were midsized or large congregations continue to shrink in size. Once upon a time they averaged 300 or 325 or 140 at worship, but a combination of factors has brought a decrease in size. In exurbia it may be new churches have raised the bar in competing for future constituents. In the inner city it may have been white flight. In some religious traditions the decline was the result of a series of mismatches in the ministerial placement process. In other cases that new building of 1921 on an adequate site at a good location has turned into a functionally obsolete structure on an inadequate site at what is now an unattractive location.

That is one source of replacements for the hundreds of small churches that disappear every year through dissolution or merger. A smaller source consists of those new missions launched several years ago that have plateaued in size with an average worship attendance of 125 or fewer. Many were intended to become large churches, but the planners used a small-church model in designing the new mission. Typically this design included (1) sending one person rather than a team to launch it, (2) choosing as that first pastor a minister who had never served on the staff of a congregation averaging more than 600 at worship and therefore had no experience with the culture and ministry of a large church, (3) defining the primary constituency to be reached and served on the basis of their place of residence rather than in terms of demographic characteristics and/or where they are on their personal faith journey and/or on their personal and family needs,

(4) selecting the mission-developer pastor or team leader before identifying that primary constituency to be reached and served, (5) affirming a relatively short tenure of one to seven years for that first mission-developer pastor, (6) purchasing a small site of three or four acres or less for the eventual permanent meeting place, (7) providing the guarantee of a large and long-term financial subsidy, thus creating a dependency relationship, (8) renting an elementary school building as the temporary meeting place for those first few years, (9) scheduling the first public worship service with an anticipated attendance under 100, (10) placing a high priority on attracting newcomers and a relatively low priority on creating a redundant system for the assimilation of newcomers, (11) reserving the role of "pioneers" for two or three or four dozen volunteers from the sponsoring church rather than drawing those pioneers from the primary constituency this new mission was created to reach and serve, and (12) placing an excessive dependence on the combination of a magnetic personality and the leadership skills of that mission-developer pastor who departs after a few years.

Those are a dozen tried and tested components of a strategy to produce a small congregation out of that new mission. Sooner or later most new missions that were designed following a small-church model either plateau in size as small churches or simply disappear from the ecclesiastical landscape.

Why Don't They Grow?

For at least three or four decades the large regional Protestant congregations in the U.S. have been attracting younger generations who in 1935, or even in 1955, attended smaller neighborhood churches. The twentieth century saw the potential service area of most Protestant congregations expand from a radius of 3 miles or less to 8 to 30 miles. (A radius of 8 miles includes seven times as much area as a radius of 3 miles.) The number of privately owned motor vehicles in America per 1,000 population, age 14 and over, doubled between 1955 and 2000. Why have so few of the small Protestant churches of 1950 or 1980 not increased in size? One useful explanation requires a change in the system used to categorize congregations.

Instead of using size to explain why churches differ so much from one another, let us back off to take a larger view of the approximately 325,000 congregations under that broad umbrella called American Protestantism. That perspective offers two other lines of demarcation that provide a better understanding of the differences among churches. The first of these two stands out most clearly when the 200,000 congregations averaging 100 or fewer at worship are compared with the 7,000 averaging more than 800 at worship.

The vast majority of those 7,000 very large churches, and an even larger proportion of those experiencing significant numerical growth, are organized around a clear persuasive unambiguous and precisely defined declaration of "This is what we believe, and this is what we teach." On a spectrum that runs from certainty at one end to ambiguity at the other extreme, most of these very large congregations are located in the third of that spectrum labeled "Certainty."

For most of them, that emphasis is focused on two subjects. The first is Christology. These congregations proclaim an orthodox statement about Jesus Christ. They proclaim that Jesus was the Son of God, he was both human and divine, he did die on the cross, he did rise from the dead on the third day, and his life and death atoned for the sins of human beings. They also believe and teach that Christ will come again. They believe and teach that we live in a world filled with sin and evil. Redemption is possible only through Jesus Christ.

The second point of certainty is in the authority of Scripture. These congregations do not raise human reason nor human experiences nor tradition to the same level of truth or guidance as Scripture. It cannot be emphasized too strongly that this focus on certainty is not only clearly defined, it also is presented in a persuasive manner that minimizes internal division. Why this emphasis on *persuasive* preaching and teaching? We live in a culture filled with highly persuasive messages from exceptionally skilled advocates of a huge variety of goods, services, views, ideas, dreams, and experiences. In order to compete effectively in the contemporary public square, anyone proclaiming the gospel of Jesus Christ must be a persuasive communicator.

A substantial number of other very large American Protestant congregations expand on what comes under the label of certainty. That list may include polity, creedal statements produced by committees of human beings, and the wall that separates the clergy from the laity. Most, however, limit their definition of certainty to Christology and the authority of Scripture. They do not pretend to speak with equal certainty on such divisive issues as dress codes, the use of alcoholic beverages or coffee or tobacco, membership in lodges, instrumental music, the role of women in the church, the age for baptism, liturgical practices, divorce, issues of human sexuality, the design of church buildings, compensation for the clergy, American foreign policy, land use controls, requirements for ordination, immigration laws, taxation, or modern technology (electricity, indoor plumbing, the use of gasoline-powered motor vehicles, radio, motion pictures, telephone, television, or projected visual images in worship).

Those congregations that decide to speak with absolute certainty on eight or more of the issues in that long paragraph usually discover that can be extremely divisive. One consequence is, relatively few of them can be found on any roster of the very large Protestant congregations in contemporary America. By contrast, most of today's very large congregations keep that list of concerns they address with unequivocal certainty to Christology and the authority of Scripture. That minimizes divisiveness and enhances the power of persuasion.

Three Big Shifts

From this observer's spectrum the second most remarkable movement of churches on that spectrum has been in regard to divorce and remarriage after divorce. In the 1950s nearly all of the very large Protestant churches in America spoke with certainty on that issue. Today most have moved to the ambiguity half of the spectrum. The third big shift during the past half century has been on the role of women in the church. Many that spoke with certainty in the 1950s on the limited role of women drifted over to the ambiguity side for a generation or two and now speak with certainty that women can and should enjoy the same rights and privileges as men in the church—since both are sinners, why separate them into two categories based on plumbing? Issues that were highly divisive only a few generations ago, such as driving a motor vehicle on the Sabbath, electricity, hymnals, lodges, motion pictures, dress codes for the clergy, seating men and women next to one another, the use of the English language in worship, or stained-glass windows are now at the extreme end of the ambiguity side of that spectrum.

The big shift, however, is rarely even mentioned, and that is why it tops this short list. With two major exceptions (Seventh-day Adventists and Seventh-day Baptists), for most of American church history nearly all Christian congregations in America spoke with certainty on this point. The first day of the week is when Christians should gather for the corporate worship of God. That was not even on the list of acceptable subjects for intradenominational or inter-congregational quarrels in 1950. Five decades later American Protestant congregations of all sizes, shapes, and labels are scheduling worship for the seventh day of the week. Scores report the service with the largest attendance is scheduled for Saturday evening—and no one challenges the legitimacy of that schedule. That represents another shift from old certainty to ambiguity to a new certainty that God is alive and at work in the world even on Saturday evening.

The basic generalization is the larger the size of that American Protestant congregation in the early years of the twenty-first century and the more rapid the rate of numerical growth, the more likely (1) it is organized around certainty in regard to Christology and the authority of Scripture and (2) those declarations of certainty are presented in a highly persuasive, rather than in a confrontational or a divisive manner. In matters of religion, certainty can be a unifying rallying point, while ambiguity often is a divisive central organizing principle. The larger the size of the constituency, the more likely ambiguity on doctrine and teaching will be divisive, and the more likely certainty, if executed in a persuasive rather than a divisive style, will be unifying. This generalization applies to both con-gregations and denominations in American Protestantism.

What's the Alternative?

By contrast, the majority of America Protestant congregations averaging 100 or fewer at worship, and the vast majority of those averaging fewer than 50 at worship, have decided not to use that certainty-ambiguity spectrum as their central organizing princi-ple since that would be incompatible with the goal of not offend-ing anyone. Instead, they usually combine three or four or more of the following characteristics as their central organizing princi-ple. This list may include racial homogeneity, language, national ancestry, kinship ties, age, marital status, long tenure of members, intimacy, an absence of complexity, genuine caring for one another, frugality, continuity with the past, predictability, denominational allegiance, love for that sacred meeting place filled with treasured memories, perhaps a long-tenured and beloved shepherd, the leadership of one or two or three family trees, a cemetery on the church grounds, local traditions, the Sunday school, the women's missionary society, growing old together, mourning the death of a member, and celebrating the ministries of those members who have responded to the call to full-time Christian service. That may be reinforced by a "Don't ask, don't tell" policy on potentially divisive issues such as Christology or the interpretation of Scripture.

The Number-two Principle

At least a few readers will argue that the number-one line of demarcation that separates the very large congregations from those averaging fewer than 100 at worship can be stated more simply. The central organizing principle of the typical small church is their primary constituency consists of the current membership. The ministry is designed to "take good care of our people."

By contrast, the numerically growing very large church usually is organized to place a high priority on identifying, attracting, welcoming, serving, and assimilating the next two or three hundred new constituents. That does oversimplify a more complicated picture. The very large congregation usually can mobilize the resources to place a very high priority on both evangelism and taking good care of today's members, while the small church usually is confronted with an either-or choice.

A common example of this distinction is when the congregation averaging 300 at worship decides to enlarge the paid staff, it may seek a semiretired pastor who will make hospital calls, visit the shut-ins, and call on elderly members who live alone. When the church down the street averaging 1,200 at worship adds staff, it may call a full-time minister of missions who will focus on challenging and equipping members to be engaged in doing ministry both in the United States and on other continents.

What's the Point?

One exurban-turned-suburban community saw its population triple between 1980 and 2000. One Protestant congregation, founded in 1976, has seen its average worship attendance quintuple from 313 in 1980 to over 1,600 in 2000. A new mission founded in 1983 with an attendance of 472 at the first public worship service now averages over 1,400 at worship. First Church, founded in 1894, was averaging 127 at worship in 1980 and now averages 103. A fourth congregation, founded in 1957, was averaging 88 at worship in 1980 and 74 in 2000.

The first of these four Protestant congregations was organized around certainty and evangelism. The second was organized around certainty and evangelism. By 1980 First Church was organized around continuity with the past, taking good care of its members, frugality, denominational loyalty, and a long-tenured pastor who was the effective and loving shepherd of an aging flock. Those first two congregations consist largely of people who are comfortable with discontinuity with the past and are new residents of the rapidly growing community. With a dozen exceptions, all of the current members of that fourth church were residents of this community before the housing boom began in the late 1970s. Several moved away during the 1970s and 1980s, and when they returned, they naturally were welcomed back into their home church, which places a high value on continuity with the past.

Why did those two smaller congregations fail to at least double in size? Two reasons. First, that would have required changing their central organizing principle from taking care of their members to certainty and evangelism. Second, that would have required redefining "how to do church" from a small-congregation model to a large church style. When faced with radical change, most institutions, like most adults, prefer continuity over discontinuity.

This distinction between organizing a congregation around taking good care of today's members, instead of a persuasive proclamation of a message based on certainty rather than ambiguity, helps to explain four other patterns in contemporary American Protestantism. First, that distinction helps to explain why 30 percent of American Protestant congregations account for at least 70 percent of the worshipers on the typical weekend. Contemporary American Christians, especially those born after 1960 who live in a world overflowing with ambiguity, prefer certainty in religion. When looking for a job, choosing a spouse, supporting a candidate for elective public office, or searching for a church home, most American adults born after 1960 place a greater weight on "What do you support?" rather than on "What do you oppose?"

Second, this helps to explain the "shrinking of the middle"; as the number of very large congregations increases, the number of small churches also increases, but the number averaging 125 to 450 at worship decreases. It is easier to retain the loyal members by emphasizing continuity with the past than to compete for potential future constituents.

Third, this is one factor among several in explaining why those religious bodies in American Protestantism that are persuasive messengers of certainty include a disproportionately large number of very large congregations and relatively few small churches in contrast to those denominations that affirm theological pluralism.

Fourth, this distinction helps to explain a few of the stresses and strains experienced by that long-tenured pastor of a congregation that was averaging fewer than 60 at worship when that minister arrived on the scene and now averages 1,200 at worship. That steep uphill road is filled with potholes and dangerous sharp curves as well as with inspiring views of a new tomorrow.

Four Exceptions

Like every broad sweeping generalization, this one is marked by exceptions. One exception is the congregation that is located at the certainty end of this spectrum, but the communication style is confrontational rather than persuasive.

A second exception is the large congregation that for several years has been proclaiming a persuasive message of certainty but that messenger has departed and the successor is either (1) more comfortable with ambiguity and/or (2) far from equally persuasive.

A third exception includes perhaps a 1,000 of those 7,000 very large congregations that place themselves in the middle of that spectrum and insist that is the explanation for their numerical growth. A more realistic explanation, however, is that congregation is organized around a high level of competence in missions and evangelism, avoids a confrontational style of communicating its core values, and enjoys the cohesive quality of a long-tenured ministerial staff.

The fourth exception is more apparent than real. This is the congregation that is located at the certainty end of that spectrum, but the central organizing principle is not on "This is what we proclaim and teach." The focus is on communicating in a relevant and persuasive manner to where the constituents are on their own personal faith journeys and holding up certainty as a desirable and highly valued destination for those on this journey. This may require three different messages in three different worship experiences every week.

Other Implications and Consequences

If the definition of a "good church" is the congregation in which the people care for the sick, mourn the death of a member, miss the absentee, rejoice when that absentee returns, and where the people value intimacy, dislike complexity, and is second only to the family as a person's most treasured social network, the maximum size is probably 35 to 40 at worship. If the cohesive forces that bind the members of that social network together are reinforced by a strict, clearly defined, and universally shared religious belief system and/or the expectation that children of all ages will be in worship and/or most of the members encounter one another several times every week (the typical small-town Protestant church), that maximum size may be expanded to an average worship attendance of 60 to 75.

If that worshiping community is able to afford, attract, and retain the services of a full-time resident leader (minister or pastor or preacher) who reinforces group cohesion, it is relatively easy for it to grow to include 150 to 225 members. (In one congregation a membership of 200 will produce an average worship attendance of 85, and in another 200 members produces an average worship attendance of 160. In those with a very high threshold into membership, that figure of 200 members may be accompanied by an average worship attendance of 800.)

In other words, the dynamics of group life, of social networks, and of human settlements suggest that the natural size of an American Protestant congregation *without* its own full-time resident leader is reflected in an average worship attendance of 40 or fewer. The greater the power of the kinship ties represented by one family constellation, the more likely that number will be less than 20.

If that congregation is served by a series of short-tenured (two to five years) full-time resident pastors, the average worship attendance usually will be in the 60 to 125 range, unless it is subsidized by the denomination. The larger the financial subsidy and/or the shorter the average tenure of pastors and/or the decision to share a pastor with one or more other congregations, the more likely that pastor will not be able to provide significant social cohesion, and therefore the average worship attendance probably will be in the 25 to 75 range.

The Impact on Ministerial Careers

Finally, the Reverend George Williams, who had spent seven years helping Congregation A grow from an average worship attendance of 85 to a new peak of 115, accepted the challenge to move to Congregation B, which had been demoralized by a serious mismatch between minister and congregation. During those three tumultuous years, nearly one-half the people had left and worship attendance plunged from 110 to 65. After six years the Reverend Williams left behind a happy and grateful congregation averaging 125 at worship. He next moved to serving as the pastor of Congregation C. It was about to have its 80-year-old meeting place displaced by a new highway. The state paid the congregation $485,000 for the property. The members contributed an additional $450,000 over three years, and one family gave a seven-acre parcel of land at an excellent location for a new church site. One result was that seven years later the congregation was meeting in a new 15,000-square-foot building, the debt had been reduced to $120,000, a committee was busy preparing plans for construction of a new second unit, and the average attendance at worship was 135.

Then came the day of decision. After 20 years and three happy and effective pastorates in three sharply different circumstances, the Reverend Williams was invited to become the senior minister of a congregation founded in 1975 and was averaging 450 at worship. The founding pastor was about to retire. One condition was that the 45-year-old Reverend George Williams would willingly inherit a staff that included a 61-year-old associate minister who planned to retire in five or six years and a 52-year-old lay director of children's ministry who had joined the staff in 1986 and who expected to continue until retirement.

What should the Reverend Williams do?

1. Decide, "Yes, this is what I've spent 20 years preparing for. I've learned what to do and how to do it. I've cultivated a leadership role and style that matches my gifts and personality. I believe what has worked for me in these first three pastorates also will work for me in this church. The only big difference is I'll be working with three or four times as many people, but I'll have two experienced veterans who know that congregation to help me carry the load."

2. Reply, "No, thanks! My specialty is serving congregations that are or should be averaging about 125 at worship. I've spent two decades developing my skills to do that, and I'm not interested in learning a new trade."

3. Debate, "This looks like the spot for an intentional interim pastorate of 18 to 36 months. Do I want to accept that role and expect to move on after a couple of years? Or could this be an opportunity for me to serve a short hitch as the unintentional interim minister while I concurrently get my on-the-job training on how to be the senior pastor of a big church? Maybe I could even succeed myself and become the permanent senior minister."

4. Reflect, "I believe I've learned how to be a lifetime learner. I know that, like a lot of other men in their mid-40s, I'm ready for a new challenge. I recognize this will be unlike any situation I've ever served in before. I understand I will have to master a new set of skills, including how to follow a long-tenured and successful founding pastor, how to work with an older program staff, how to do big church right in the new millennium, and how to be the successor in a congregation that has never learned how to welcome a successor. I also understand that my predecessor was at the top of the local seniority list, and I will be at the very bottom

of that local seniority list the day I arrive. That means part of my predecessor's authority came out of a highly effective ministry, part out of seniority, and part out of the office. All my authority as the new senior minister will have to be earned. I understand that, and I accept it. Most important, I do not believe God would have placed this challenge before me if he did not believe I could do it. Therefore, with God's help and my wife's approval, I am accepting this invitation."

What do you believe should be Reverend Williams's response?

CHAPTER FOUR

THE 21ST-CENTURY CONTEXT

A s we begin to plan for the future of our congregation in this new millennium, perhaps our first step should be to survey our community and attempt to identify the unchurched population," suggested the 56-year-old volunteer leader chairing the first meeting of the newly created Futures Committee at Bethany Church, a congregation founded in 1921.

"That's important and I believe we should do that," agreed the one former Roman Catholic in the group, "but I believe our first step should be to gather the data describing the distinctive identity, the role, the goals, and the ministry of every Christian congregation serving this community. We may find some gaps that we can fill."

"I'm not disagreeing with either one of you," declared the oldest person in the room, "but my first question is, do we here at Bethany have a future? Church attendance last year averaged about 85, and that is less than half what it was when I joined back in 1971. Are we needed? It seems to me the number of churches around here is increasing, but the number of happy agnostics and atheists is increasing at a faster pace. People are going to soccer games, to the parks and beaches, to the shopping center, and to visit grandma on Sunday morning. Is there really a need for a church like this one?"

"That's a good beginning point for our discussion," responded the chairperson. "First of all, maybe those agnostics and atheists should be identified as our primary constituency as we plan to increase our evangelistic outreach. Last week I read a book that reported a Gallup poll in 1947 revealed that 89 percent of the American population, age 18 and over, identified themselves as Christians. That was 89 percent of a population of 97 million, age 18 and over, or 86 million Christians. A similar poll by the Gallup organization in 2001 found that 82 percent of Americans, age 18 and over, identified themselves as Christians. Eighty-two percent of 211 million comes out to 173 million. Thanks to the combination of the increase in the American population and longer life expectancy, the number of self-identified Christians in this country has doubled during my lifetime. Other surveys indicate that at least one-third of those self-identified Christians do not have an active church affiliation. Instead of focusing on atheists and agnostics, maybe we should make reaching the unchurched believers our number-one goal. What do you think?"

This conversation introduces two points. First, every effort at planning for the future requires a clearly defined beginning point. The list of possibilities is endless and includes problems, dreams, reacting to external forces, money, evangelism, the initiatives of a recently arrived pastor, denominationally generated goals, a shortage of offstreet parking, the aging of the membership, or the resignation or retirement of the current minister.

The second issue is what could be a relevant and productive beginning point as the small Protestant congregation begins to plan for ministry in the 21st century.

For the policy makers in the small and predominantly Anglo-Protestant congregation founded before 1965, a useful beginning point may be to take a brief look at several changes in the American church scene during the past three or four decades.

A Dozen Changes in the Context

1. The Emergence of Regional Institutions

Tens of thousands of Protestant congregations in America were founded to serve as nationality and/or neighborhood churches. The driving assumption was this church would serve a constituency residing within a 3-mile radius of the meeting place. In recent years neighborhood institutions have been replaced by newer ones designed to serve a regional constituency. That long list includes public high schools, grocery stores, physicians' offices, motion picture theaters, variety stores, public parks, financial institutions, restaurants, stores, pharmacies, funeral homes, and churches.

2. The Competition Is Greater

The competition among hospitals for patients, among grocery stores for customers, among colleges for students, among automobile manufacturers for buyers, and among airlines for passengers is greater than ever before in American history. A parallel trend is the increase in the competition among the churches for future constituents.

This increase in competition is not only for the customers' loyalty but also for people's time, attention, energy, and money. Soccer leagues, television, recreation, and shopping now compete for people's time every Sunday morning.

3. The Consumer Is More Influential

The combination of the emergence of large regional institutions plus this increased level of competition has enhanced the power of the consumer. Today's competitors recognize the need to adjust schedules to fit the convenience of the constituents. One example is the increasing number of churches that offer Saturday evening worship.

A second is the choice from among two or three or four different worship experiences on Sunday morning. One of the most significant consequences of this shift from a producer-driven economy to a consumer-driven culture is in what traditionally has been called education. Most universities are being forced to shift their focus from research and teaching to learning.[1] Naturally, this has encountered substantial resistance from professors who had specialized in talking and testing. One consequence is, degrees are being replaced by certification. Likewise, physicians frequently are offering patients a choice among Therapy A, Treatment B, and Medication C.

In the churches, the traditional Sunday school hour is being replaced by the creation of learning communities, book circles, and two-hour weeknight or daytime learning experiences. Instead of inviting a missionary to come and show a series of slides, teams of adults spend 7 to 15 days working with fellow Christians in a sister church on another continent.

4. Expectations Are Greater!

As recently as the 1950s public schools were expected to educate children and youth and to help them master the social skills required to get along with other people. Today, public schools also are expected to feed and clothe the students; to administer prescribed medications; to provide surrogate parents; to monitor the physical, mental, and emotional health of students; to operate a complicated transportation system; and to prepare them to earn athletic scholarships to universities.

Likewise the expectations parishioners bring to church are greater in number, higher in the level of quality required to meet them, and more varied in the range of events, activities, and choices.

5. Institutional Loyalties Are Weaker

Patriotism flourished during World War II. The 1940s were marked by a strengthening of loyalties to institutions. The beneficiaries included the military services, service clubs, the public schools, colleges and universities, fraternal organizations, large corporations, and religious bodies. Lutherans were loyal to their western European religious heritage. Catholics were loyal to the Roman Catholic Church, and tens of millions of American-born Christians inherited their religious loyalty from their parents.

One example of the erosion of denominational loyalty is this: for 1956 the 39,845 Methodist churches in America reported they had received 309,760 new members by letter of transfer from other Methodist churches. For 1999, however, the 35,609 United Methodist churches reported they had received only 115,908 new members by way of intradenominational transfers.

The 1960s brought a culture filled with disillusionment. One facet was disillusionment with the traditional institutions of American society. That list included military organizations, institutions of higher education, profit-driven corporations, patriotic events, government, white-dominated racist systems, and male-dominated religious traditions. That list also included many of the traditional religious structures and organizations, such as Sunday school and the missionary organizations for women.

Institutions in the 21st century are expected to earn and re-earn the loyalty of their constituents. That generalization applies to retailers, professional sports teams, political parties, commercial airlines, the Roman Catholic Church in America, government, automobile manufacturers, the mainline Protestant denominations, and congregations.

One of the highly visible consequences of this combination of regionalism, competition, consumerism, rising expectations, and the erosion of institutional loyalties is American Protestant congregations, like professional football players, grocery stores, pickup trucks, milk bottles, teenagers, single family homes, post offices, television sets, farms, stomachs, motion picture theaters, hospitals, closets, paperclips, soft drink bottles, universities, bathrooms, lawnmowers, parking lots, and bookstores, are larger than they used to be. The number of Protestant churches in America has increased by no more than 40 percent since 1955, but the number averaging more than 1,000 at worship has quadrupled.

At the other end of the size scale, the number of very small Protestant congregations also has increased. The result is a shrinking middle. Many of the denominationally affiliated congregations that averaged between 75 and 800 at worship in the 1980s have shrunk substantially in size. A relatively tiny proportion have grown to beyond 800 in worship attendance and are able to mobilize the resources required to compete for future constituents. A disproportionately large number of today's megachurches were founded after 1960. That generalization applies to white, black, and Asian churches in America.

The erosion of denominational loyalties, the diminishing number of adults who worship with the congregation they were born into decades earlier, the demand for relevance, quality, and choices, the increased difficulty of finding a new pastor who can bring the gifts, theological stance, skills, personality, potential tenure, experience, work ethic, priorities in ministry, and leadership required for an excellent match with the needs of that congregation at this point in its history, the easy drive to a church 5 or 10 miles away from home, and that rapidly growing number of interdenominational and interfaith marriages have placed tens of thousands of midsized American Protestant congregations on the list of endangered religious organizations.

While hundreds of small Protestant churches in America disappear every month through mergers or dissolutions, they are being replaced by a larger number of what formerly were midsized to large congregations that have shrunk in size to fit into the small church category. Are small churches a disappearing breed? No. Their names are changing, and their numbers are growing.

6. The Criteria for Self-identification Are Changing

For most of American history, up through the first half of the 20th century, three of the primary lines of demarcation among the residents of America were skin color, place of birth, and ancestry. These three lines of demarcation were clearly reflected in the divisions among American Christians, in political parties, in the definition of neighborhoods, in journalism, in employment opportunities, and in other aspects of life in the United States.

In 1955, Will Herberg's book *Protestant, Catholic, Jew* was published.[2] Herberg argued that religion had replaced ancestry as the primary criterion used by Americans in defining their own individual identity. One evidence of this was the public debate over John F. Kennedy's candidacy for the presidency in 1960. Another was the mergers of several Protestant denominations that previously had projected a clear western European identity such as Swedish Lutheran or German Methodist. A third was the Americanization of religious traditions such as the German Baptists, Swedish Evangelicals, German Evangelicals, Dutch Reformed, or Swedish Baptists.

In the 1960s, however, the combination of ecumenism, individualism, consumerism, and interfaith and interdenominational marriages began to erode the influence of religion as the primary criterion for self-identification. This issue became more complicated as a consequence of the new waves of immigration that came, not from western Europe as had been the norm through the 1920s, but from Asia, Latin America, and Africa. For a substantial segment of the American population, skin color, place of birth, and ancestry once again became influential criteria in individual self-identification. September 11, 2001, also lifted up religion again as a significant line of demarcation.

Consequentially, nationality, native language, skin color, place of birth, and inherited religious loyalties again are powerful forces in church planning. Planning a new Presbyterian mission to serve people who recently migrated from Korea to America as adults requires a different design from that used in planning a new mission to reach American-born residents who are the children of parents who were children when they came here from Korea.

Likewise a different design is needed for the new mission designed to include fourth or fifth or sixth or tenth generation American-born blacks who identify themselves as integrationists than is appropriate for the new mission to reach self-identified African American or Afro-American separatists.[3]

Perhaps the most significant consequence for the vast majority of predominantly white Protestant congregations in the United States is the erosion of denominational affiliation as a central component of that church's identity. Exceptions do exist in varying degrees. The Seventh-day Adventist Church, the Jehovah's Witnesses, the Southern Baptist Convention up through the 1980s, the Orthodox Presbyterian Church, and the Religious Society of Friends (Conservative) are among the exceptions.

The most highly visible example of this basic trend, of course, is that rapidly growing number of nondenominational megachurches. A second is the growing pressure for schism in several denominations.

For many denominationally affiliated white Protestant congregations, however, their community image tends to focus primarily on one or more of these characteristics: (1) its theological stance, (2) the demographic characteristics of the majority of its newest constituents, (3) the numerical increase or decrease in worship attendance, (4) the personality and gifts of that long-tenured pastor, (5) an institutional specialty such as a Christian day school, the operation of a home for battered women or an extensive recreation ministry, (6) a focus on one or two stages of the personal faith journey of individuals, (7) the visibility of that congregation on television, (8) a reliance on a multisite strategy to proclaim the gospel of Jesus Christ to larger numbers of people, and/or (9) its dependence on lay leadership rather than on the clergy.

The contents and strategies of this book are intended primarily for white Protestant congregations composed largely of people whose ancestry traces back to Europe and who are more comfortable in English than in any other language. A different set of strategies and tactics are required in those congregations in which skin color, place of birth, a reliance on a language other than English, and/or ancestry are highly influential forces in the self-identification of the constituents.

For example, the Lutheran congregation founded in 1908 as a nationality parish that by the 1950s had evolved into a congregation of American-born and English-speaking members may have difficulty on its 100th anniversary in attracting and assimilating recent immigrants from Mexico, Korea, India, China, or Central America who now constitute the majority of residents of that neighborhood. It is far easier to relocate to a community populated largely by American-born and English-speaking residents whose grandparents also were born in the United States.

7. From Egalitarianism to Individualism

During the 1940s and 1950s, the American culture placed a high value on freedom. The 1960s brought a new era in which many concluded egalitarianism should be the highest cultural and political value. One subsequent expression of egalitarianism was an affirmation of diversity. The pressures to increase diversity were most highly visible in American higher education, in employment policies, in the judicial system and, to a lesser degree, in several of the mainline Protestant denominations.

The 1990s brought a renewed emphasis on individualism. What came to be identified as "radical egalitarianism" was perceived as a threat to individual rights.[4] One example was the legal battles over the admission policies of tax-funded state universities. Recent public opinion polls suggest the majority of adult Americans (and nearly all 2-year-olds) rank individual rights above egalitarianism or the goal of greater diversity.

For this discussion the most relevant example of individualism is that large number of Christian churchgoers who switch religious traditions when they change their church affiliation. A highly visible example consists of those young third- or fourth-generation American-born "cradle Catholics" who are now worshiping with a Protestant congregation. Another is the 13-year-old daughter who shocks her father by the new clothes she recently purchased to wear to school. A third is the congregation that sends most of its benevolent dollars directly to ministries of its choice rather than channel those dollars through denominational treasuries.

Where do these values of egalitarianism, diversity, and individualism rank in the design of the ministry plan for your congregations for the 21st century?

8. From Integration to Ethnic Separation

The most subjective of the dozen trends discussed in this chapter is also the most politically sensitive. The 1960s brought a wave of support for the racial integration of the Christian churches in America. Four decades later only modest progress has been made to achieve that goal.

Why so little progress? One reason clearly was and is white racism. Another was and is black separatism. A third was the unspoken but widely shared assumption that the road to the racial integration of the Christian churches would parallel the roads to the racial integration of the American armed forces, to the racial integration of the public schools, to the racial integration of employment opportunities, and to the racial integration of the historically white colleges and universities. Blacks would be welcomed into white institutions. Most of the burden of initiating change would be placed on black Americans.

What would have happened if, instead of merging the overwhelmingly white Evangelical United Brethren Church into the predominantly white Methodist Church, those two committees on church union would have recommended dissolving both denominations and urging each congregation to petition for membership in one of the three black Methodist denominations?

What would have happened if, in the mid-1980s, instead of uniting three Lutheran bodies into one new denomination—with the goal that by 1997 10 percent of the members would be persons of color or persons whose native language is not English—the decision had been made to urge all congregations to apply for affiliation with a Korean or African American or other ethnic religious body?

If, in planning for the future of a congregation or denomination for the 21st century, the policy makers place a high value on racial and/or ethnic integration, should that road be designed for ethnic minorities to join predominantly white organizations?

Or, should it be designed for whites to join organizations created by and consisting largely of an ethnic minority?

9. The Continued Impact of Technology

The combination of the invention of movable type and the translation of the Scriptures into the language of the people revolutionized Christianity in Europe. More recently the railroads, paved roads, and widespread ownership of the private motor vehicle, and electricity have transformed rural America and changed the context for ministry for tens of thousands of rural congregations. Add in the changes in mining and agriculture from labor-intensive to capital-intensive industries, and it is easy to explain the existence of so many aging and numerically shrinking congregations founded before 1960.

More recently television has raised the bar in terms of what is an acceptable level of competence in communication, made obsolete the assumption that worship should be conducted in black and white, and provided nearly every churchgoer a model of a high-quality and inspiring worship service. In scores of communities, cable television has provided interested congregations with direct access to thousands of living rooms. The Internet has enabled interested persons, without leaving home, to look in on any part of the world and visit churches by plugging into that congregation's website. Videotapes have enabled any interested congregation to be inspired and challenged by superb sermons delivered by exceptionally competent communicators.

A more extensive discussion in chapter 10 describes how small congregations can improve and expand their ministry by taking advantage of these technological miracles.

10. From Scarcity to Abundance

For generations a widely shared and highly influential assumption was that by definition small Protestant congregations were severely limited by a scarcity of resources. They were short of people. Often they also were limited by a low ceiling on financial resources. Many operated with a shortage of informed, committed, and highly skilled volunteer leaders. Others were limited by a shortage of creativity.

One of the dramatic changes on the American ecclesiastical scene is the growing number of small Protestant churches that have received a gift from a living donor or a bequest from a deceased member of somewhere between $100,000 and $3 million. The affluent economy of the last quarter century did not lift every ship in the harbor, but it did raise the financial ceiling in literally thousands of small Protestant congregations.[5]

The number of adults living in rural, urban, or suburban America who display a high level of leadership skill and/or an abundance of creativity is at least quadruple what it was in the 1950s. Those small churches that are limited by a shortage of competent and creative leaders usually can, if they wish, "borrow" volunteer lay leaders from a self-identified missionary church (see chapter 6). This should be especially easy in denominations with a presbyterian or episcopal system of governance.

Creating a ministry plan based on a context of abundance produces a different design than one based on an assumption of the scarcity of resources. A persuasive argument can be made that this change in the context is both the most widely neglected and also the most influential factor in planning for the future of the small church in American Protestantism.

11. The Southern Wind

While the state of contemporary Christianity in western Europe is widely discussed and is a useful reference point for the prophets of gloom and despair, a more relevant reference point in planning for the 21st century is the health, state, vigor, and growth of Christianity in the Southern Hemisphere.[6] The winds of change from the Southern Hemisphere, and from the Pacific Rim, already are making an impact on the American religious scene. A simple example is the number of Christian missionaries coming to the United States from the Southern Hemisphere and from the Pacific Rim probably exceeds the number coming from western Europe by a 1,000-to-1 ratio.

One consequence already is being experienced by those American Christian bodies that see themselves as part of a larger global religious system. That list includes Anglicans, Roman Catholics, and Lutherans. The members of these religious bodies in Africa, Asia, and Latin America usually see themselves as theologically more conservative than their counterparts in Europe and North America. They are more likely to focus their worship on the second or third persons of the Holy Trinity, while their northern brethren are more likely to exalt the first person. This becomes a major line of demarcation not only within a single religious tradition, but even more so in efforts to promote ecumenism. That southern wind also brings a renewed emphasis to the north on mysticism and puritanism, along with a higher priority on evangelizing nonbelievers.

The 19th-century history of American Christianity includes scores of schisms and denominational divisions. The 20th century includes the stories of dozens of denominational reunions and mergers. What will the 21st century bring? That southern wind may fan the fires of schism that already are smoldering in several American religious traditions. How do you take that into account in designing a ministry plan for your congregation?

12. When the Big Gorilla Rolls Over?

September 11, 2001, made it clear to anyone who still had doubts that the United States has become the most influential nation in the world in terms of the economy, military power, political influence, and the export of cultural values. The export of those cultural values was clearly a primary motivation behind the terrorist attacks of 9/11. One consequence of that is one-half of the residents on this planet who choose to move to another country migrate to the United States. Tens of millions more would love to follow.

On the American domestic scene, one debate is over redefining the doctrine of the separation of church and state. While that debate continues, civil governments are expanding their role and invading what once was assumed to be among the responsibilities of the Christian churches. For most of American history, hospitals, colleges, homes for children, and similar charitable and philanthropic ventures were created, financed, and administered by the churches. Today, for every penny American Christian churches collect for operating hospitals, children's homes, and educational institutions, the federal government provides several dollars. State and local governments add more dollars to the funding. Religious organizations such as Catholic Charities, the Salvation Army, and Lutheran Social Services collect billions of dollars annually from the federal government.

For most of American history religious congregations picked the site for construction of their meeting place without any form of permission from state or local governments. Today, land-use regulations and building codes influence the location, size, design, and pace of construction for houses of worship.

This is not a plea to return to the political and economic marketplace of 1880 or 1955! It is a plea, however, to recognize that the actions and policies of government may have a huge impact on designing a ministry plan for your congregation for the 21st century.

Do you plan to expand the size of your meeting place? Will that mean the entire building will have to meet the requirements of the current building code? Do you plan to open a weekday Christian elementary school? How will it be funded? Out of the congregation's budget to give the parents a tax break? Or by tuition? Or by tax-funded vouchers? Or will it be a charter school? Are you planning to create an endowment fund for your congregation? If so, should that be a legally incorporated foundation or trust? Or controlled by the trustees of the church? Are you contemplating relocation of your meeting place? What will be required by that unit of local government for you to secure approval to remove that parcel of land from the tax roll? To overcome opposition by neighboring property owners and residents? To secure a building permit? To secure an occupancy permit? What types of outdoor lighting can be used for the parking lot and soccer field? If you decide to enlarge your present meeting place, what are the restrictions that will be placed on future use of the property? If your plans are rejected, are you prepared to litigate? Or to yield?

This is far from an exhaustive review of the changing context for ministry in America, but the changes described here do illustrate a central theme of this book. It is far more important, and also far more difficult today, for the small Protestant congregation to design its own customized ministry plan than it was in 1955 or 1985.

CHAPTER FIVE

SUPERSTAR OR TALENTED TEAM?

One of the most divisive issues in contemporary American philanthropic circles is over what to subsidize. One side of this debate acts on the assumption that the United States has a shortage of individual leaders. Back in the 1966–1977 era, the Ford Foundation invested more than $11 million in a nation-wide effort to identify 700 individuals who appeared to possess the gifts and commitment to become influential leaders. These individuals displayed a relatively high level of personal initiative and a commitment to improving their schools and/or the communities in which they lived. A customized program was designed for each person chosen. The central goal was to provide the experiences, travel, tools, skills, challenges, and opportunities to rethink their career plans that would transform potential leaders into influential leaders by enriching their individual lives.[1]

More recently the Ford Foundation has funded international programs designed to enhance the gifts and skills of potential leaders in other parts of the world. In 2001 it funded a $28 million worldwide program designed to provide graduate scholarships over the next 10 years for individuals who will promote social and economic justice in all parts of the world. The Rockefeller Foundation funds an extensive program in individual leadership development. Perhaps the best-known contemporary focus on individual leaders by a foundation was launched by the John D. and Catherine T. MacArthur Foundation in 1991. Two dozen individuals each received a $500,000-no-strings-attached fellowship in 2002. The Lilly Endowment has allocated tens of millions of dollars to improve the quality of leadership among parish pastors.

The other side of this debate contends the most urgent need is to encourage the creation and equipping of leadership teams. The Robert Wood Johnson Foundation is an example of a philanthropic organization that is committed to equipping teams.

The Ecclesiastical Scene

The historic emphasis in American Protestantism appears to be on the individual leader rather than the team. Perhaps the most widespread example consists of congregational leaders who are convinced, "If we could only find a pastor who is a real leader, our church would flourish." At least a couple of dozen theological schools have created a faculty position for a professor who will concentrate on helping students become more effective leaders. For at least three decades leadership has been a major theme in designing continuing education events for pastors. Several denominations have made this a high priority.

This raises what may be the most divisive issue discussed in this book. Is America in general, and the Christian churches in particular, confronted with an unprecedented shortage of talented individuals? This is a recurring theme when the discussion focuses on candidates for the presidency of the United States, or the search for a new chief executive officer of a large profit-driven corporation, or a replacement for the departing superintendent of a public school system, or the successor for a denominational executive, or for the next pastor at Old First Church.

One perspective contends the issue is a shortage of talent. The other side argues America enjoys an abundant supply of talented leaders, but most institutions are not organized to nurture, embrace, and take advantage of the gifts and skills these talented individuals bring to their assignment.[2] Most readers will agree we have a national shortage of superstars. Where are the successors to Martin Luther King, George Washington, Thomas Edison, Franklin D. Roosevelt, or General George C. Marshall? On the contemporary American religious scene, Leith Anderson has earned a reputation as an exceptionally wise senior minister and interventionist. Robert Schuller has enjoyed a long career as one of the most innovative and visionary parish pastors in American church history. Rick Warren deserves to be called "America's most influential pastor."[3] For a quarter century Bill Hybels has provided outstanding leadership for America's best-known megachurch,[4] and Howard Edington has modeled the leadership role for a downtown church in Orlando;[5] while Claude E. Payne[6] and B. Carlisle Driggers[7] stand out as exceptionally effective regional denominational executives.

Despite these and other success stories, American Christianity continues to experience a shortage of superstar clergypersons who can come in and produce one miracle after another. The demand for superstar ministers exceeds the supply by at least a 40-to-1 ratio. That suggests most small congregations would be well advised to add the option of teams to their list of alternative scenarios.

While this observer is convinced the primary problem is most of the ecclesiastical institutions in American Christianity were created in an era that called for individuals, rather than egalitarian teams, to provide the required leadership, that is not the issue here. That is a systemic problem, and we do know how to redesign existing dysfunctional systems. That is another story for another day.

The issue here is that the options available to the 100-year-old congregation averaging 35 at worship, which has shared a series of a dozen pastors with another congregation over the past 40 or

50 years, do not resemble the options open to the congregation averaging 1,000 or more at worship.

At the large church end of the size spectrum, an increasing proportion of very large congregations are choosing to build long-tenured leadership teams. One model calls for the successor to the old pattern of the senior minister who occupied a solitary box at the top of the organizational chart to be succeeded by a three-to-five person team of full-time people. A typical team, for example, includes two ordained ministers who share the preaching, the program director, the executive pastor (who may or may not be ordained), and one specialist such as the minister of missions. One of those five also acts as the team leader.

A different design calls for a team of teams. Each ministry area is staffed by a team, typically one or two or three paid staff members (either full-time or part-time), plus two to eight lay volunteers. The leaders from each team share in that weekly staff meeting.[8]

Ordained Minister or Talented Lay Team?

The first question for most small Protestant congregations is, Do we want a loving shepherd or a visionary leader who is an effective agent of planned change initiated from within the congregation? Or, do we want to ask a missionary church to send us a team of free agents as described in chapter 6? Those small churches that place a high value on serving as a surrogate family, on caring for one another, on maintaining continuity with the past, on intimacy, and on the absence of complexity, tend, if they believe they have a choice, to opt for the loving shepherd.

Some will argue the first question is, Do we want, can we economically afford, and can we attract a full-time resident pastor?

Chapter 6 is based on the assumption that high on that list of alternatives most small churches should give serious consideration to the possibility of being served by a team of gifted lay free agents who have been identified, challenged, enlisted, empowered, and equipped by a missionary church. That option expands this list of questions from one or two to at least eight. The second, and most important question is, Who will issue that invitation? A representative from the regional judicatory of that denomination? The departing part-time minister? Three-to-five of the most widely respected and influential volunteer leaders? Or, does this require a unanimous vote at a congregational meeting? That missionary church should respond affirmatively only to valid invitations!

It is relatively easy for the five or six full-time members of a new team in that very large congregation, with the enthusiastic and informed support of a dozen respected and influential volunteer leaders, to replace the old system with a new one. That old system was designed as a hierarchy, with the senior pastor alone in a box at the top of the chart showing the staff configuration. When that minister departs, along with those staff members who are either unable or unwilling to become members of a more egalitarian team, the new team usually has an open road to introduce and adopt that new organizational model.

That paragraph introduces the third of these eight questions. Who has the authority to discard that old clergy-centered system and replace it with a new model when that missionary church (described in chapter 6) responds to an invitation to send a team of three to five equipped free agents to fill the role that had been filled by a succession of part-time ministers? That missionary church? The leaders who issued the invitation? An interventionist on the staff of the regional denominational judicatory? That team of free agents? One of the most effective ways to produce a high level of frustration is to ask someone to fill a vacancy that does not exist at this time in that particular organization.

Fourth, and perhaps this should be first, is the polity of your denominational system open to and will it be supportive of the use of these teams of talented lay free agents to fill a role historically reserved for ordained ministers? Or, should this scenario be reserved for those religious traditions that have a long history of a wide open door to lay leadership or to nondenominational congregations? If your denominational system is largely controlled by the clergy, will these talented lay free agents be permitted to preach, to lead worship, to administer the sacraments, to officiate at weddings and funerals, and to vote at denominational meetings? Will the door be open to eventual ordination? To serve as full-time paid professional ministers? Or will the system send a message to the congregation: "This is the best we can do for you now, but we look forward to the day when we will be able to help you find a real minister." Will that message be overheard by this talented team of free agents?

Fifth, should the successors to the initial members of that team be drawn from the members of that congregation? One argument for this pattern is the indigenous leaders probably will have a deeper and more comprehensive understanding of the distinctive culture of that particular small church than will be possessed by outsiders.

Or, should the successors to those initial team members also come from that missionary church? One argument is they bring an outside perspective plus experiences that help them lift up a vision of what tomorrow could bring.

Sixth, what if this doesn't work for us? Who has the authority to initiate the process that will terminate this relationship? That group of volunteer leaders who issued the invitation to that missionary church? The governing board of that small church? The members of that lay team? A handful of discontented members? The minister of missions at that missionary church?

A seventh question is raised by the option of the larger parish (see chapter 9), which is designed for one team of professionals to serve several small churches. Is that the best option to produce the outcomes we desire?

An eighth question is raised by those congregational leaders who have concluded, "We don't need a loving shepherd. Four of our lay volunteers have completed the training provided by the Stephens Ministry, and we have our own volunteer worship leaders. We have a good team consisting of our own people. We don't need a visionary leader. Our goal is to perpetuate today. All we really need that we don't have is top-quality preaching every Sunday morning." What is the best way to fill that vacuum? A retired minister? An ordained minister who is teaching in a college or seminary? Videotapes? A stream of guest preachers? Rent one of the associate ministers on the staff of a megachurch? A seminary student? A certified lay preacher? A seminary graduate who is in five-day-a-week secular employment?

Two Other Scenarios

Occasionally a different scenario raises a potentially divisive issue. One example is the small church that is served by a full-time pastor who combines excellent preaching with the gifts and personality required for the loving shepherd. Ever since that minister arrived, this congregation has been experiencing gradual numerical growth. Last year it averaged 121 at worship, up from 89 six years ago. An outsider was invited to evaluate their situation and suggested, "Given the increase in the population in this area, if you relocate and construct new facilities on a larger site at a better location, you could triple in size in 10 years."

The pastor clearly and openly is not interested in that option. "I do not possess the gifts and experience required to pull that off."

What should be done? Replace that loving shepherd with a visionary leader? Give their loving shepherd a three-month sabbatical to master the skills required to be a visionary leader? Discourage first-time visitors from returning? Search for two or three of the free agents described in chapter 6 and encourage the pastor to invite them to help create a new leadership team. One person could be the part-time program director responsible for expanding the group life in order to accommodate additional people. The other could carry the staff responsibility for the relocation. A different but not uncommon scenario surfaces in those religious traditions that have a century or two of dependence on volunteer teams, rather than paid clergy, for congregational leadership. What should we do when a combination of circumstances causes our average worship attendance to jump from 35 or 50 or 60 to well over 100? A useful first step is to visit two or three

Mennonite, Brethren, Quaker, or similar congregations that have gone through similar experiences and learn from them.

These two scenarios introduce what really should be the first question on this agenda. Agree that staffing is a means-to-an-end issue and postpone discussion of it. Focus first on what the leaders in that congregation agree God is calling that congregation to be and to be doing five years down the road. What does that mean in terms of such means-to-an-end issues as schedule, real estate, governance, finances, staffing, and community image?

The parallel pattern is in denominational policy-making meetings where officials place a high priority on how to staff small congregations. A better beginning point would be to identify the desired outcome that denominational system is expected to produce. Subsequently, focus on how staffing can produce the desired outcomes.

CHAPTER SIX

EMPOWER THE LAITY!

The first item on the agenda often influences the content of the subsequent discussion. What is the crucial problem facing most small Protestant congregations in America today? A common response to that question is a shortage of highly competent seminary-trained pastors who are both able and eager to provide the ministerial leadership these congregations seek.

A more productive response asks the "Why?" question. Why do we have that shortage? One answer is most of today's American-born white seminary graduates do not come from a small-church background, and even fewer were reared in rural America or in the inner city. The drop in the American farm population from 30 million in 1940 to fewer than 4 million today has sharply reduced one source of seminary students. Another explanation for this shortage is compensation.

The Compensation Package Is Larger

While most readers will agree this is a means-to-an-end issue, the simple fact of economic life in the United States is the cost of fully credentialed and full-time parish pastors has increased at a faster rate than the increase in the Consumer Price Index. During the past 45 years, the Consumer Price Index rose from 28.9 in 1958 (1982–1984 = 100) to 185 in 2003 or slightly over a sixfold increase. During those same 45 years, per capita personal income in the United States increased fifteenfold, or two and one-half times the rate of inflation.

The total compensation (including cash salary, housing allowance or rental value of church-owned parsonage, payment by the church for utilities, auto allowance, pension, health insurance, continuing education, book allowance, and so forth) for the typical full-time and fully credentialed American-born Protestant parish pastor of western European ancestry in 1958 was approximately $3,600 to $8,000. (The total compensation for most black pastors and immigrant ministers was lower than for American-born white clergy in 1958.)

That range of $3,600 to $8,000 is a consequence of the differences in compensation for pastors in the various Protestant traditions and regional variations. The median of approximately $5,000 was for full-time resident pastors who had earned a seminary degree and were serving a midsized congregation averaging 135 to 150 at worship. The total compensation for ministers serving smaller congregations usually was less.

How much is $5,000 after adjusting for inflation? In 2003 the equivalent buying power was approximately $32,000. One solution to the problem of staffing small churches with seminary-trained clergy is to increase the number who are willing to serve for an annual cash salary of approximately $10,000 to $15,000 plus housing, utilities, health insurance, the congregation's share of pension payments, auto allowance, and other fringe benefits.

If, however, that increase in per capita personal income is used as the multiplier, 15 times $5,000 comes out to $75,000. In many urban and suburban communities where the rental value of a four-bedroom single-family home may be $15,000 a year plus $3,000 for utilities, $8,000 for health insurance for the family, $4,000 for auto allowance plus $3,000 for the congregation's share of pension payments, the 2003 equivalent of that 1958 total compensation comes out to at least $65,000.

The cash salary of pastors serving small and midsized Protestant congregations has not climbed at an exorbitant rate. It has increased at approximately the same rate over the past 45 years as the increase in per capita personal income—but part of that increase in per capita personal income is a result of the increase in the number of two-income families, and part is a consequence of a sharp increase in the number of persons with a very high income.

The *big* impact on congregational budgets has not been in cash salaries, it is in the cost of fringe benefits. In 1958 it was almost unheard of for a congregation to pay for health insurance for the minister and the minister's family. Likewise most small and midsized congregations did not pay the cost of utilities for the parsonage nor did they include an item in the church budget for continuing education or for a book allowance. Many did not compensate their pastor for car expenses, and a large number did not pay anything into the minister's pension account. In many communities the cost of housing has increased at a far faster rate than the increase in per capita person income.

One alternative for the small Protestant congregation in America is to relocate to a Third World nation where fringe benefits are not a significant component in the pastor's total compensation.

Challenge the Free Agents

A far more productive approach places a different question at the top of the agenda. Instead of focusing on the rising cost of fringe benefits, a better question is, "What other changes in the American labor force can have a beneficial impact on the future of the small church? As we change our approach to the future from planning on the basis of a shortage of resources to planning on the basis of an abundance of exceptionally valuable resources, where should we focus our attention?"

Instead of looking at the ministerial marketplace, focus on another slice of the American population. Today, the American population includes an unprecedented large number of adults who share these 12 characteristics.

1. They were born before 1960, and many were born before 1950.
2. They enjoy excellent physical health.
3. They are mentally sharp.
4. An unprecedented proportion have earned at least one college degree. Many have completed more years of formal education than the typical parish pastor.
5. Most significant of all, a large number have experienced a series of successes in life. These may include education, marriage, parenthood, hobbies, secular employment, and a variety of roles as a volunteer in nonprofit institutions. They bring a record of success to their plans for the future.
6. They have chosen early retirement from the secular labor force and/or they have accumulated sufficient wealth that "making a decent living" no longer is a driving force in their lives.
7. They are deeply committed Christians.
8. They have both benefited from and enjoyed their volunteer responsibilities as an active member of a worshiping community.
9. They have demonstrated they are persons of good moral character.
10. They possess the gifts and competence required for congregational leadership.
11. They have mastered the art of lifetime learning and are eager to continue to learn.
12. They are waiting to be challenged to use their time, talents, and experience in serving Jesus Christ through his church.

The term "free agents" has been used to describe these adults who are too young, too energetic, too healthy, and too eager to help create the new to be comfortable with the concept of retirement.[1] An estimated 200,000 Protestant congregations in the United States average 100 or fewer people at weekend worship— and that number does not include the thousands of unincorporated house churches that meet in private homes. More than one-half of those 200,000 reported a decrease in worship attendance during the 1990s.

What does the future hold for them? One response has been to dissolve. A second has been to merge with another congregation. A third has been to receive a denominational subsidy to enable them to employ a resident pastor. A fourth has been to look to a seminary student for part-time ministerial leadership. A fifth has been to turn to the semiretired minister for part-time leadership. A sixth has been to share a pastor with one or more other small churches.

This chapter is devoted to a course of action that could be a productive road into the future for the majority of these 200,000 small churches, if they believe in the ministry of the laity.

What Do You Believe?

The beginning point for designing this strategy is an assumption that does not have universal support. This basic assumption is that for the majority of these small congregations the influential variable in determining their future will not be their denominational affiliation. Many do not carry a denominational identity and for most of those that do, this denominational label clearly has not attracted a flood of newcomers. This key variable will not be their location or their real estate or how long that church has been in existence. It will not be the age of the current constituency, nor the budget, nor the Sunday school, nor the women's organization.

The key variable in shaping the future of at least 100,000 of these 200,000 small American Protestant congregations will be leadership! If you do not agree with that assumption, you have wasted your time reading this far.

A second guiding assumption was introduced as point 10 back in chapter 4. American Christianity today enjoys an unprecedented abundance of gifted, skilled, experienced, creative, and deeply committed leaders. One portion of this abundance of leadership is found among the clergy. A far larger quantity, however, is found among the laity. The issue is not availability, it is a willingness to identify, challenge, enlist, empower, equip, place, and support potential lay leaders. Many readers will contend that adult females represent at least 60 to 70 percent of these potential lay leaders, but we will not be diverted by that issue in this chapter.

A third assumption, which also is seen by many as a divisive issue, is these deeply committed, gifted, and experienced laypersons can, if permitted and equipped, provide every facet of leadership required by these small congregations. That list includes leading the process to plan for the next chapter in that congregation's history, preaching, counseling the troubled, administering the sacraments, preparing budgets, officiating at weddings and funerals, enlisting volunteers, raising money, chairing meetings, visiting the sick, ministering to shut-ins, proclaiming the gospel to the unchurched, representing that congregation at denominational gatherings, partnering with sister churches on other continents, and teaching and challenging other laypersons to identify and use their gifts in ministry.

One reason this appears to be a safe assumption is, we have nearly 2,000 years of history in the Christian church of the laity filling all these roles. A second reason is the laity are engaged in these expressions of ministry all over this planet today.

A conservative estimate is the current American population includes at least 12 million adults who are deeply committed Christians, regular participants in the corporate worship of God, and active members of a Protestant congregation. That does not include another 40 million irregular attendees who for one reason or another are absent from worship at least seven or eight weekends every year. Assume that 97 percent of those 12 million regulars do *not* display all 12 of those characteristics described earlier in this chapter. That leaves 360,000 who do display all 12 characteristics. If properly challenged, that could produce more than 100,000 teams of two to five free agents who could be enlisted and equipped to provide the ministerial leadership required by one-half of those 200,000 small churches.

Finally, a fourth assumption should be seen as a fact of contemporary life in America, *not* as a motivation for adopting this strategy. With relatively rare exceptions they cost less. Many have a comfortable retirement income. Others have a part-time or full-time secular job. A substantial number are not in the labor force, but are married to a full-time wage earner. A fair number are widowed and waiting to be challenged. Some require a modest stipend for their time. A common practice is reimbursement for all out-of-pocket expenses, plus a modest stipend.

Several free agents who do not need the money do require the congregation to pay them a reasonable stipend for their time and energy. One reason is to minimize the temptation to "let Pat the volunteer do it." The goal is to challenge, not replace, indigenous volunteer leadership. The big reason, however, is to minimize the possibility of pauperizing the congregation with free professional help.

Five Policy Questions

The above paragraph introduces the first of five policy questions that merit serious discussion. Each one has at least two sides to it. Future misunderstandings and problems can be minimized by winning widespread agreement on each policy issue before opening this door to these contemporary Christian free agents.

1. Insiders or Outsiders?

A persuasive argument can be made on behalf of the value of indigenous leadership.[2] The long-term goal can be to encourage local indigenous leadership in every small church. One strategy for reaching this goal is for that initial team of two to five outsiders to be guided by two long-term objectives. One objective is the team will strive to leave behind when they depart a congregation that displays the four missionary characteristics of a church that is self-expressing (it has defined its own distinctive identity and role), self-governing, self-financing, and self-propagating.

The second long-term objective is that each team will identify, enlist, and equip a successor from among the constituents of that congregation. Usually this means replacing members of that team one-by-one over a period of a year or longer. That enables the veterans on the team to mentor each replacement on a one-by-one basis as they join the team.

A different, more expensive, and far more difficult strategy is for the regional denominational judicatory or a retreat center or a parachurch organization to offer training experiences for current members of small churches to prepare them to be competent, self-confident, and committed indigenous leaders of that congregation.

The most serious deficiency in that approach is the temptation to design a shoe that will fit every foot in those training programs. By contrast, when that team of outsiders spends a year or more as leaders in that congregation, they are more likely to follow a customized approach in identifying, enlisting, and equipping the indigenous leadership for that particular congregation.

The number-one reason, however, for beginning with a team of outsiders is that requires an invitation from the congregation. The members of that small church *must* take the initiative! Instead of bemoaning the shortage of pastors willing to accept their invitation, that small congregation must accept the responsibility for initiating a new approach. That opens the door to planned change initiated from within that fellowship.

That option of "sending our own people" to be equipped often feeds the hope that tomorrow can be a repetition of yesterday.

An essential core value of every team of free agents is, "We won't go unless we are invited." That may substantially reduce the number of small churches choosing this option, but it is a crucial component of an effective strategy.

The second reason for enlisting outsiders is the other side of the coin for not inviting current members to carry this responsibility. If the goal is a congregation that is self-expressing, self-governing, self-financing, and self-propagating, that initial team should consist of adults who come from a congregation that displays all four of those characteristics. That means the sending congregation probably will average at least 135 to 150 at worship. In real life experience suggests most teams of free agents come from that 4 percent of American Protestant churches averaging 500 or more at worship, which together account for approximately 30 percent of all the people worshiping with a Protestant congregation on the typical weekend. Instead of that lay team being guided by past experiences in a small church, it is more helpful that they be guided by experiences in what tomorrow could bring.

A third reason for building these teams of lay free agents from invited outsiders is they are more likely to be driven by a vision of the future rather than by memories from the past. That combination of being invited, of bringing a fresh outside perspective, and of introducing a strong future orientation, plus their absence of obligations to kinfolk or long-time friends can produce a favorable climate for change.

Finally, a fourth argument for building teams of outsiders is generated by the question, What happens if this doesn't work? Mismatches do occur. Personality conflicts do arise. Sometimes the rhetoric favoring a new era is overcome by the weight of local traditions. What does that indigenous team do? Enroll in an advanced class-in-conflict resolution? That team of outside free agents can urge, "In retrospect, this was a mismatch. We will leave, and we will pray that the next team you invite will be a good match."

2. Individuals or Teams?

During the past 50 years, American Protestants have accumulated a vast quantity of experience in (1) sending a part-time lay pastor in to serve a small church, (2) inviting a full-time minister to serve, and hopefully transform, a small congregation, (3) relying on seminary students to serve as the weekend pastor of one or more small churches, (4) asking a full-time minister to serve two or more churches, and (5) turning to semiretired ministers to serve as part-time pastors of small congregations. The first four of these alternatives have produced a disproportionately large number of short pastorates, dissolutions, mergers, disillusioned clergypersons and lay pastors, numerically shrinking congregations, adult children of members who continue to live in that community but have chosen a full-service church elsewhere for their family, and endless denominational financial subsidies, both direct and indirect.

That team of three to five lay free agents comes with a half dozen advantages. Together they represent an alliance. It is not one person alone against "all of them." Second, three different personalities will enjoy an easier time enlisting allies from among the constituents than will any one person. Third, three heads not only are better than one, together they also bring more brains, gifts, skills, relevant experiences, and wisdom than any one person could bring. Fourth, the team functions as its own mutual support group in those crucial early weeks. Fifth, if one person is absent, the hole is only one-third the size as when that solo performer is absent. Sixth, the disruption created by permanently replacing one member of a three-person team is far less than when the one-person "team" departs and must be replaced. (See chapter 5 for a longer discussion of this issue.)

3. Where Is the Support System?

The individual coming to serve as the pastor of a small church, either part-time or full-time, may be able to turn to a sympathetic spouse for support, but usually has to build a support system from among the members. A few years later the successor may have to build a new but somewhat different support system.

The three- to five-person team comes with two advantages. First, the team functions as a system for its members. Second, the sending church usually provides a backup support system.

4. Are We Allowed to Comparison Shop?

For most of American history, marriages involved a man and a woman who were reared in the same or adjoining counties. World War II changed that pattern. It is not uncommon today for the bride and groom to have been born and reared in two different states, or even on two different continents.

For most of American history, people were taught the world offers us two choices: take it, or leave it. Adults content with that range of choices today tend to be found in retirement centers, nursing homes, and cemeteries. The generations born in America after World War II were reared in a culture that taught them they are entitled to a broad range of attractive choices. That thinking turned out to be contagious, and thousands of parents caught it from their teenagers.

The chances that staffing small churches with teams of lay free agents will produce desirable outcomes is greatly increased if the congregational leaders can declare, "We interviewed three or four teams, and you folks are at the top of our list." The chances of success go up another notch if that team responds, "We looked at four other churches seeking a team, and this congregation is at the top of our list." Arranged marriages are incompatible with the contemporary American culture.

Real-life experiences with this concept over the past four decades suggest a slightly different shopping pattern. The self-identified missionary church enlists and equips a team of lay free agents to provide the leadership for a small church. This turns out to be a highly visible success story. One consequence is that once the operational model has been created and can be visited, it becomes much easier to enlist volunteers for additional teams. Most of us normal people prefer to be in the second group to implement a new idea rather than to serve as the pioneers.

The second consequence is success breeds curiosity. Leaders in other small churches visit this working model, talk with the people, are impressed by their enthusiasm, go back home, talk about it, and conclude, "Let's try it." They send a delegation to go knock on the door of that missionary church and ask, "When could you send us a team of lay free agents?" That introduces the fifth of these five policy questions.

5. Who Carries the Ball?

One scenario calls for the pastor of that missionary church to introduce this concept, to enlist, and to equip that team of lay free agents and to answer the door when leaders from small congregations come knocking. The big deficiency in that scenario is most pastors are limited to 168 hours per week. How much time can the pastor spend building, equipping, placing, and supporting these teams and in answering the door?

That question introduces three reasons that most of these missionary churches are larger than 95 or 96 percent of all other Protestant congregations in America. One reason is the availability of these free agents. The larger the congregation, the greater the number of free agents. A second reason is the larger the size of the congregation, the less likely most of these free agents have to be "creamed off" to fill vacancies for volunteers in that church. A surplus of resources makes it easier to help others.

The crucial variable, however, is small and midsized congregations tend to teach ministers "Your job is to do ministry." By contrast, the senior pastor of that large and numerically growing congregation probably has learned, "My key responsibility is not to do ministry. My job is to make sure ministry happens." That attitude creates the culture required to make this scenario available to thousands of small churches.

One consequence of that stance is one of the fastest growing staff positions among large Protestant congregations in America is the minister of missions. At least two dozen different job descriptions have been written under that title. For example, in one congregation the primary responsibility of the minister of missions is planting new churches. In another it is to build alliances with sister churches on other continents and to enlist and lead teams of short-term missionaries to work in ministry with fellow Christians in those sister churches.

A third definition of responsibilities is to lead in the creation and staffing of off-campus ministries. One version is to plant new worshiping communities designed to reach and serve unchurched adults who rarely are found in the conventional approach to congregational life. The Key Church Strategy invented by Southern Baptists in the 1970s provides a superb tried-and-tested model of this scenario.[3] In this pilgrim's travel, Tillie Burgin at the First Baptist Church of Arlington, Texas, stands out as an extraordinarily inspiring, creative, and effective model of a minister of missions for this scenario.

A different scenario is the one described in this chapter. This places three major responsibilities on the minister of missions. One is to identify, challenge, screen, enlist, empower, and equip free agents to serve on these teams. A concurrent responsibility is to identify, evaluate, and prepare those small churches that believe their future will benefit from this scenario.

A critical variable in determining the future success of this specialized ministry is in the selection of the first two or three small congregations that ask the missionary church to provide them with a team. If these turn out to be winners, that almost guarantees the future success of this scenario. It also increases the probability the line of small congregations knocking at the door of that missionary church will grow longer year after year.

That introduces the central responsibility of this role for a minister of missions. This includes (1) creating internally cohesive and mutually compatible teams out of those volunteer free agents, (2) matching the gifts, skills, and priorities of those teams with the needs of the appropriate congregation, and (3) providing a continuing combination support and learning environment for those teams and the congregations they serve. In real life this means the minister of missions occasionally must explain to a new team, "At the moment, we do not have a congregation in waiting that would be a good match for you," and/or to a congregation knocking at the door, "Right now we do not have a team that matches your needs, but give us time and we may be able to create one for you."

That matchmaker responsibility never ends and is time-consuming, especially if it includes encouraging congregational leaders to interview at least two or three teams before issuing an invitation and encouraging each team to evaluate at least two or three alternative assignments before accepting a particular invitation.

Caution!

This traveler's experience suggests it is easier for a carefully selected team of church planters to launch a new mission that is averaging at least 350 at worship by the end of the third year than it is for one minister to revitalize a numerically shrinking congregation that has been growing old and passive for the past decade or two.

Likewise, enlisting and equipping a lay team of free agents to provide the required ministerial leadership for a small congregation established before 1975 is a radically different assignment than asking that team to create a new worshiping community from among unchurched adults.

CHAPTER SEVEN

THE AFFILIATE
RELATIONSHIP

W hat are the options for the small congregation averaging somewhere between 35 and 100 at worship in which the members place a high value on (1) enjoying the intimacy, the caring, the spontaneity, the friendships, and the absence of complexity and anonymity that often are central components of the culture of the small church, (2) continuing to gather for worship in what had become a sacred and comfortable place filled with wonderful memories, (3) being fed spiritually by superb preaching that combines a high level of excellence in communication with persuasive, meaningful, and relevant content, and (4) cultivating the ability to attract and retain the allegiance of newcomers to replace the members who die, move away, or drop out?

That size bracket includes approximately one-third of all American Protestant congregations. What are their options?

One is to create an endowment fund of $2 million to $3 million. (See chapter 10.) The annual income from investments should enable that small church to maintain the real estate and also to attract and retain the services of an excellent preacher. A

93

second is for every member household to return to the Lord through that congregation's treasury a full tithe of their annual income. Ten of those tithes will be used for the pastor's compensation and the remaining tithes can be used to cover operating expenses. A third is to share a pastor with another congregation. A fourth is to share the costs of maintaining that sacred meeting place with another congregation. (See chapter 9.) Another alternative is to look to the missionary church described in the previous chapter and invite a team of lay free agents to accept the responsibilities of ministerial leadership.

The Affiliation Model

A parallel but different model begins with the self-identified missionary church that opens the door to requests for affiliation by smaller congregations with the values described in the opening paragraph of this chapter. The name of this type of missionary church may be found on the grapevine, on the Internet, or on a list that is kept up-to-date by the regional judicatory, or a national office of that denomination, or by a parachurch organization.

This affiliation model of the missionary church is based on six assumptions. First, the demand for biblically based sermons that carry a persuasive message of hope and certainty founded on God's grace and the love of Jesus Christ has never been greater than it is today. Second, television has raised the bar of what qualifies as effective communication. That bar is now several notches higher than it was in 1960. What earned a grade A for "excellent communication" by a public speaker, professor, preacher, or candidate for national elective office in 1960 now receives a grade B −. Third, one consequence is a severe national shortage of ministers who combine relevant and high-quality content with excellent skills in communication.

The fourth assumption is far more divisive. This assumption declares that after 40-plus years of training, the vast majority of the American people are now comfortable watching and absorbing messages delivered by way of moving visual images projected on a screen. Motion pictures, television, videotapes, and computers have moved projected visual images right behind touch, facial expressions, gestures, and one-to-one eye contact as the most effective channels of communication. The spoken word delivered directly by a speaker to a crowd may be a distant seventh (behind one-to-one conversations), but it is no longer among the top five, if one counts both the quality of the impact and the quantity of communication. In other words, radio is not as powerful as television in communication in the contemporary American culture.[1]

At least three dozen American preachers and at least four or five seminary professors strongly disagree with this fourth assumption. They contend that it is essential the preacher know the people for whom that message has been prepared and that it be delivered in person. One exception is the preacher substituting for the pastor who is on vacation. A second is the denominational official who is the guest preacher for one day. A third is when a candidate arrives to deliver a trial sermon. A fourth is the new minister who arrives on Thursday and is the preacher of the day on the following Sunday. A fifth exception is the guest preacher at the seminary graduation ceremony, or a denominational meeting, or an interfaith worship service. A sixth is the part-time intentional interim minister who serves during a pulpit vacancy. A seventh is the pulpit exchange arranged by two parish pastors. An eighth exception is the television preacher who delivers the message to hundreds of thousands of people watching and listening at home. A ninth exception is the senior pastor of the megachurch who may be able to call correctly by name one-tenth of the worshipers in that particular service. A tenth is the audiotaped sermon listened to by someone while driving his or her car to work. The biggest exception, of course, consists of those clergy who have published books of sermons without ever meeting most of the people who will read those sermons.

Another big exception is that adult class studying a book written by a person who has never even visited that state and has never met anyone in that class. A common example is the class studying a book written by a white male who died long ago named Mark, or a book written by a man named Luke.

This point of view is supported by the complete absence of any historical data showing Jesus, Paul, Martin Luther, or John Wesley ever relied on radio, television, or videotapes to proclaim the gospel. Handwritten letters and printed channels of communication apparently are acceptable, but electronic channels are not acceptable to these purists.

A completely different response is revealed by shifting from an ideological to a pragmatic perspective. Will Christians come to a church that has replaced the live preacher with a videotape? A new nondenominational Protestant congregation in Rockford, Illinois, celebrated their first anniversary in July 1999 with two firsts. For the first time in history their worship attendance exceeded 1,400. That also was the first time in their history they had ever had a live preacher. In Edmond, Oklahoma, the use of videotapes has enabled Life Church to offer 10 weekend worship experiences at five different locations with a combined total worship attendance averaging over 6,000. That is above average among new missions founded in 1996!

In a small community in suburban Chicago in March 2001, a relocated congregation was averaging fewer than 50 at worship with a live preacher on Sunday morning. A year later, with a videotaped message replacing the live preacher, their worship attendance exceeded 400. What produced that dramatic increase? In late 2001 they requested affiliation with a multisite missionary church. A fifth assumption (for those who are still counting) reflects a radical change in the larger American economy. The specialist has replaced a generalist. That change can be seen in the practice of medicine, the practice of law, the practice of teaching, the practice of agriculture, perhaps most clearly in professional football, and in hundreds of other slices of the American economy.

In the old American ecclesiastical economy, the parish pastor was expected to display an acceptable level of competence as a preacher, administrator, pastor, counselor, evangelist, teacher, youth director, worship leader, fund-raiser, and, ideally, musician.

Today's megachurches build a staff of specialists. How does the congregation served by one pastor who is a generalist compete for potential future constituents with that growing number of megachurches staffed by highly skilled specialists? One response is to turn to teams of free agents, each of whom brings a special competence as described in the previous chapter. Another response is to carve out a niche and excel in that niche. (See the following chapter.)

This fifth assumption declares a Christian congregation does not have to produce all of the resources it requires. That has been true for many decades. Protestant churches have been depending on others to create for their use hymnals, Sunday school materials, candles, pews, translations of the Bible, and dozens of other resources. The videotaped sermon is simply one more resource from outside in that long line of resources created by others. Depend on specialists to do what they excel at doing, and the generalists will utilize resources created by others.

Finally, a sixth assumption is this: geographical distance is not the barrier it once was. Rather than affiliate with one or two other geographically nearby congregations to form a two- or three-church parish served by one minister, today it is relatively easy to affiliate with a congregation that matches our congregation's theological stance, our values, and our culture.

Seven Models

One model of this strategy calls for the missionary church to provide autonomous congregations with two or three resources. One is that carefully edited videotape of the message for next Sunday's worship service. That may be a carefully edited videotape made the previous Saturday evening at the missionary church. It may be a videotape of the previous week's sermon. It may be a videotape chosen by the leaders of that small church from a selection of dozens of videotapes. The date that message was first delivered usually is less important than the continuity represented by the person of the messenger and far less important than the relevance or quality of the message. In several congregations the edited version begins with a customized greeting delivered by that messenger to a particular congregation.

The second resource in that model is the missionary church provides a continuing training program for 3 to 10 volunteer worship leaders from that small congregation. That training program focused on (1) equipping these volunteers to lead that congregation in the corporate worship of God, (2) advising them how to design a customized worship experience that is a good match for both the people who will be present and that particular physical environment, and (3) teaching them how to utilize that videotaped message in worship.

In the ideal circumstances that small church schedules Sunday school to follow worship. An adult class, which may include teenagers, is organized around a structured discussion of that morning's message. The missionary church provides customized study guides for each videotaped message, plus "hands-on" training for volunteers from that small church who will lead those classes. The key assumption behind this is borrowed from Professor K. Patricia Cross and others who have been evaluating teaching and learning in institutions of higher education.[2] Learning is greatly enhanced if the students can benefit from interactive "feedback" and discussions immediately following the presentation. She urges each student to be expected to prepare a one-minute paper in response to two questions: What is the big point you learned today? What is your big unanswered question? Today many ministers include two or three of these open-ended questions in the bulletin to help parishioners gain more from that sermon. This can be adapted to provide two or three customized questions for each videotaped message. Creativity is enhanced if those questions are printed in the bulletin and are used to introduce the discussion in the class following the worship service.

A second model reduces the expectations placed on the volunteer leaders in that small church. The team of lay free agents described in the previous chapter bring the videotaped messages. This relieves that team of the responsibility for preparing and delivering the sermons. That may make it easier to assemble the team.

Both of these models are designed to support the autonomy of that small church. The current members retain the power of self-governance and also continue to carry the full responsibility for maintenance of their meeting place and other operating costs.

A third model often originates after one of the first two evolves from affiliation into a courtship. After two or three years of a happy relationship, utilizing one of these two models, the leaders in that small church inquire, "How can we continue this relationship, but also guarantee that we will be able to continue to worship God at our sacred place? You have other ministries in which our people would like to participate, but we don't want to give up our own place. How can we do that? Can we have our cake and eat it, too?"

If the real estate owned by that small congregation is compatible with this model, the answer may be, "Instead of your merging with us and selling your property, you could become our west campus. We currently operate with our central campus, plus a north campus where we now offer three worship services every weekend, and an east campus where we rent space in a strip shopping center to serve the students at the community college. We do this under one name with one message, one staff, one governing board, one budget, one treasury, and one identity, but with three sites. If you wish, you could become our west campus, and we will reserve one place on our governing board for you."

What often has become the crucial negotiating point in this model relates to title to the real estate. The missionary church usually offers an either-or option: "If you want to continue as a separate legal entity and retain a clear title to your real estate, you must carry all the financial responsibilities that entails. If you want to tap into our treasury for the maintenance of this west campus, title to the property must be transferred to this legal corporation."

This third model may or may not use videotaped messages at the west campus. One of the staff of the missionary church or a lay preacher may serve as the live messenger at that site.

A fourth model sometimes is described as the "wounded bird" strategy. What once was a healthy and vital congregation has fallen on hard times. The congregation owns a good building on an adequate site at an attractive location, but worship attendance has dropped from a couple of hundred or more to fewer than a hundred. This may have been the product of a series of short pastorates or an internal and highly divisive feud or one or two serious mismatches between minister and congregation.[3]

Frequently, this is the story of what decades earlier was created to be a neighborhood church serving people with a western European ancestry. As the decades rolled by, the original residents were replaced by American-born blacks, or by immigrants from Latin America or Asia, and/or by newcomers from a different social class. As their numbers continued to shrink, the members narrowed their options to five: (1) relocate the meeting place to where their members have been moving, (2) redefine their role from a neighborhood congregation to a regional church and acquire the land for parking required for that new role, (3) replace the departing Anglo pastor with an ethnic minority minister who will "reach the people moving into this neighborhood," (4) merge with another congregation in a similar situation, or (5) continue to talk rather than to act. Since none of the first four options are able to gain the support of more than one-third of the membership, the fifth is chosen by default.

Eventually the remaining members turn to a missionary church with the plea "Help us! Will you provide us with the leadership we need to become a viable congregation once again?"

The missionary church agrees to become the senior partner in a temporary arrangement. The strategy calls for identifying and agreeing on a primary constituency, designing a ministry plan to serve that primary constituency, and implementing that plan. Five years later, worship attendance has passed the 150 level. That wounded bird has recovered, and is able to terminate the affiliation as it regains the capability to be a self-expressing, self-governing, self-financing, and self-propagating worshiping community.

The fifth model parallels the fourth, except in this case the wounded bird is a new mission launched several years ago that now averages fewer than 100 at worship. Their experience has demonstrated once again that long-term denominational subsidies may not be the most productive therapy for this type of wounded bird. The missionary church, which has mastered "how to do big church in the 21st century," takes over the wounded bird and imparts those skills into the culture of this new mission—which often was launched using a small-church design.

The rarest, but potentially the fastest-growing, version of the affiliation model is illustrated by this comment: "It sure is good to be back home! We spend the summers at our cabin and, while we're there, we go to this small church. About half of the people are permanent residents, and about half are summer people like we are. We've been told that in the winter, attendance drops to about 50 or 60, but in the summer the church is close to full. The minister is a real nice person but, at best, an ordinary preacher. We enjoy our time at the lake with our neighbors, most of whom also are summer residents, but we look forward to coming home to be inspired and renewed by some great preaching."

The details vary. One refers to a winter in a retirement center in the Sunbelt, while another describes five winter months on a Florida beach; and a third spends the summer in a second home in the mountains. This pattern is the product of the recent increase in the number of American families who own two homes.

This sixth model calls for the missionary church to take the initiative in building an affiliation with a small congregation in that community by the lake, or in the mountains, or in the Sunbelt. A more daring strategy is for that missionary church to open a second (or third or fourth) campus in that community. How can people enjoy the continuity of the same messenger when they go to their second home? One response is to combine the gifts of free agents with the magic of videotapes.

Finally, a seventh model is now on that table surrounded by denominational policy makers. The key assumption is that in the contemporary American culture many people find it easier to build a loyalty to a person than to an institution. Every four years about one-third of the American voters cast their ballots for the nominee of the Democratic Party for president, nearly that many vote for the Republican nominee, and the others vote for the candidate they prefer. Most high school and college students can name their favorite academic course, but the majority find it easier to identify their favorite teacher.

The arrival of videotapes has opened the door for every congregation to benefit from excellent sermons delivered by superb communicators. One inevitable consequence that already is apparent is the relationship between the individual viewer and the messenger. We now have 40 years of experience with television watchers developing a strong loyalty to their favorite television preacher. In tens of thousands of those experiences that relationship has grown into a channel for the transfer of money from viewer to messenger. Far more important, that relationship also has become the foundation for propagating a particular theological perspective.

Advocates of a complete free market in religion will applaud, and a few may even suggest, "Give people choices! Why not encourage congregations to use a videotape from an evangelical preacher at the first service on Sunday morning. Choose a videotape from someone in the middle of the theological road for the second service, and pick a videotaped sermon by a theological liberal for that third service."

The denominational policy maker may bring a different perspective to this discussion: "We agree with the value of giving people choices, but we also want to reinforce loyalty to our denomination. One way we can do that is to invite several of our very best preachers to prepare and deliver the messages to be delivered by way of videotapes. Some of them are in congregations that possess all the technical skill required to produce network-quality videotapes. Others may seek our help. We will focus on marketing these. Some churches may prefer to use the same messenger every week, while others may choose a series by one of our ministers, followed by a series by a different pastor from our denomination. We also will provide the resources needed by those teams of lay free agents and by those Sunday school classes organized around feedback on that morning's sermon."

An alternative scenario calls for every self-identified missionary church to accept the full responsibility for resourcing other congregations, including the design, production, and marketing the required training events, videotapes, instruction manuals, study guides, and support systems.

Does that suggest that the religious scene in America is becoming simpler, or more complicated? One response to that question is, increasing the number of meaningful choices usually raises the level of complexity. That also raises the level of frustration among those who demand, "Why can't you give a simple either-or answer?"

CHAPTER EIGHT

CARVE OUT A NICHE

Two months before I graduated from seminary my wife and I were invited to come and serve this congregation," explained the 26-year-old minister of the Oak Grove Church founded in 1909 as a rural farming community church. "As you can see, this end of the county is being built up as part of exurbia. Most of the newcomers commute 10 to 30 miles to work every morning, but they moved here because the price of homes is lower, thanks to lower land costs. Many also wanted to combine country living with a city paycheck. The year before we arrived, church attendance averaged 83. We've been here nearly a year, and we're now running close to 90. One reason we accepted the invitation is the leaders made it clear that I could and should reserve one-third of my time for evangelizing the unchurched people living out here. About four months after we arrived, I made appointments to visit the pastors of each of the 11 other Christian churches, including the one Catholic parish, serving this part of the county. In each visit, I inquired what their worship attendance was currently. The combined total for all 12, including the Oak Grove Church, added up to slightly over

4,200. The population for the area served by these churches was nearly 13,000 in April 2000. That suggests there are a lot of unchurched people out here!"

Who Are the Unchurched?

While this young pastor left out one part of his assignment—learning what could not be taught in seminary on how to be an effective parish pastor in that particular environment—this sounds like a promising arrangement. This congregation will provide the minister with a full-time compensation package for what is really a two-thirds time workload on condition the other third of his time is devoted to evangelizing the unchurched. The one big remaining question is the strategy to be followed to evangelize the unchurched. What would be the ideal strategy for this pastor in this setting?

The answer is, "That depends." The first big line of demarcation is, should this pastor unilaterally design and implement a strategy? Or, should this pastor enlist three to seven lay volunteers, and together they will design and implement a strategy? That is a premature question.

A prior question: Which slice of that unchurched population will constitute the primary constituency for that strategy? While not everyone will agree with this ranking, this observer's experience suggests the unchurched population probably includes at least these 16 cohorts or groups. They are listed in order from those most likely to be easy to reach (identified first), and those most difficult to reach (listed last).

1. Recent newcomers to this area who are Christian believers and are searching for a new home but have yet to find it, and who come from the same denominational tradition as this pastor.
2. Ditto, but come from a different religious heritage and are still searching.
3. Ditto, found it, but are not joining.

4. Ditto 1 and 2, but these newcomers thought they had found their new church home. Several months after finding it, the pastor departed, and they are deeply discontented with the successor. The result is last week they began a new search.
5. Married couples who are newcomers, who were reared in two different religious traditions and "never got around to going to church after we married." They moved out here as new parents. They identify themselves as Christian believers. The wife is now a "stay-at-home mother," and they have agreed "the time has come for us to get back to church."
6. The married couple, both of whom are self-identified Christian believers, consist of one spouse who was born and reared here who married an "outsider." The "outsider" insists, "I'm willing to go to any church you choose as long as it's not the one your family attends."
7. The Christian believers who are newcomers but are seeking a congregation that worships in their native tongue rather than in English.
8. The family who are Christian believers, who worshiped with the Oak Grove Church the first Sunday after they moved here and left completely convinced, "This is not the church for us." They are still looking for a compatible church home.
9. The family of believers who moved here recently and are still looking for "a church that uses the kind of music we prefer."
10. The agnostic who was reared in a believer's family, became an agnostic, married another agnostic who also was reared in a believer's family, and recently decided the time had come for them to set out together on a spiritual quest for truth and certainty in a world filled with ambiguity.

11. The adult children of resident agnostics or atheists who are on a self-defined personal faith journey, but have yet to find a church home.
12. Locally born and reared teenagers who resemble the adults in 11.
13. The newcomers who were born and reared in Christian church-going families but recently have had one or two extremely disillusioning and bitter experiences in Christian churches and have concluded that a person can be a good Christian without ever going to church.
14. The newcomers who are happy agnostics or atheists.
15. The long-time residents who are contented agnostics.
16. The long-time residents who are contented atheists.

It would be easy to expand that list to four or five dozen. One addition, for example, could be the parents who are looking for a church that operates a Christian day school or has an exceptionally attractive ministry with older teenagers.

That is not the point. The point of that list is the more precise the definition of "unchurched," the easier it will be to design and implement a strategy to reach the unchurched. Instead of attempting to reach and serve everyone, the leaders in small Protestant congregations should consider carving out a distinctive niche.

What Is a Niche?

For this discussion the definition of a niche is a distinctive identity or role or constituency. This can be illustrated by several examples. One church specializes in serving families created by an intercultural marriage. The number-one symbol is the pastor is in an intercultural marriage. Another congregation affirms the rights of women. The number-one symbol is the current pastor is female. A third church specializes in serving home schooling parents and their children. One symbol is the pastor is a home schooler. One evidence of this specialty is four or five afternoons every week, home schooled children gather at the church for a variety of learning and socializing experiences. This is an especially attractive niche for the small congregation because many home schoolers prefer the intimacy and absence of complexity of small institutions. Another congregation's distinctive identity is the half dozen athletic teams that compete in church leagues. Several congregations in the West and Southwest have carved out a niche as a "cowboy's church."

A church in Texas that was averaging a dozen at worship called a 19-year-old as its new pastor. Within months attendance had more than tripled. Several small churches schedule two worship services every Sunday morning, one designed and staffed by teenagers. A completely different version of this concept is illustrated by several congregations that have recreated the traditional Wednesday evening prayer meeting on Sunday morning.

One of the most interesting specialties is the small church that is experiencing substantial numerical growth, thanks largely to an influx of mature adults. The outsiders attribute this to the fact the congregation owns a reconditioned long distance passenger bus that makes 40 trips a year ranging in length from one day to a weekend to eight or nine days. A better diagnosis is based on the assumption that most Americans begin to lose their ability to meet and make new friends about their 30th birthday. Thirty years later their social network has shrunk substantially. Those trips are designed to make it easy for lonely adults to meet and make new friends. In one of these, the pastor noted, "That bus now produces six or seven weddings year after year after year."

Several small congregations recruit and equip teams of 5 to 10 mature adults every year to go and spend a week or longer working in ministry with fellow Christians in a sister church on another continent. Hundreds, perhaps thousands, of small congregations enlist and provide a support system for volunteers in mission in nearby public schools, public park programs, nursing homes, hospitals, or retirement communities.

Two of the most popular specialties that are offered by congregations of all sizes are symbolized by their slogans. One is, "We're here to help you rear your children." The other is, "We're here to help create healthy, happy, and enduring marriages."

Perhaps the most common niche is filled by the thousands of congregations averaging 8 to 35 or 40 at worship that provide a warm, caring, and supportive surrogate family for people living alone. (See chapter 3.)

What's the Point?

The last half of the 20th century saw the generalist replaced by the specialist. Instead of bemoaning the shortage of fully creden-tialed ministers able and willing to serve that small congregation, the leaders might ask themselves, "What is our distinctive niche among all the churches in this larger community? What are the unmet needs that we have the resources to respond to effectively? Could our future lie in defining a specialized area of ministry to reach and serve a slice of the population currently overlooked by the other churches around here?"

The crucial point that cannot be emphasized too strongly is that these are *not* church-growth strategies! Numerical growth may be a consequence, but that is not the driving motivation. The driving motivation is to direct the power of the Christian faith to the transformation of lives by responding to unmet needs.

CHAPTER NINE

QUESTIONS ON SHARING RESOURCES

Compensation for a minister and maintenance of the meeting place, including utilities and insurance, are the two largest items in the budgets of tens of thousands of small American Protestant congregations. As a result, one consequence of diminishing numbers and rising costs is to share a pastor with one or more other congregations. A second alternative is to share the use of that meeting place with another congregation and/or with one or more community organizations. One common example of the shared meeting place is to rent space for use by an immigrant congregation. Another is to house a weekday child care or preschool program. A third is to rent space to a parachurch organization, a denominational agency, or a community organization.

A completely different approach to sharing resources has many adherents. This calls for cooperating with one or more other churches in specific ministries. That long list includes the cooperative vacation Bible school; a joint youth ministry; shared worship services during Lent and Advent, and on Thanksgiving,

Christmas Eve, or September 11; and union services on Sunday morning during July and August while the pastor of each congregation takes a month's vacation, or on Tuesday evenings for an adult Bible study program.

A Common Question

Should this sharing of resources be a recommended component of a larger strategy for small churches? One answer is, that depends. First of all, most proposals to share resources such as real estate or a minister are motivated by a widely held assumption there is a scarcity of resources. That, of course, was a valid assumption in 1933 or even, in many communities and congregations, in 1983. Whether that is a valid assumption for any one particular congregation in the early years of the 21st century deserves serious consideration.

Many readers, however, will prefer to begin either by planning based on the assumption there is a scarcity of resources or by looking at the pluses and minuses of sharing resources. If the long-term goal is the eventual merger of these two or three congregations, sharing resources and ministries can be a productive element of the courtship. If the primary motivation is to produce larger crowds of participants from these cooperating congregations, this may be a good idea, but the basic arithmetic usually resembles this pattern. If a unilateral approach would produce 15 participants from Church A, 20 from Church B, and 25 from Church C, the joint effort probably will attract 30 to 40 participants. On the other hand, if the driving goal is to provide a community witness of ecumenism and a cooperative spirit, these joint efforts may illustrate that attitude.

If, however, the goal is to identify, attract, welcome, serve, and assimilate future new members, cooperating in shared ministries can be counterproductive. The most obvious reason is it blurs the distinctive individual identity of each participating congregation. More important, if each of the events and ministries is designed to provide an attractive entry point for newcomers to "our church," the power of that invitation is eroded by the natural tendency to focus on encouraging participation by members of each of the cooperating congregations. It also makes it difficult for those first-time visitors to decide, "Is this the church for me?" Equally significant, if the real estate or the people or the leaders at the host church create a negative image in the minds of these first-time visitors, that negative image may be attached to all the participating congregations.

Potentially the most subversive of these approaches to sharing resources often follows the decision to share the meeting place with another organization. The most obvious benefit is income to help pay for the maintenance and operation of the real estate.

On the downside this may enable the leaders to postpone designing and implementing a future-oriented ministry plan. That additional income offsets the loss of income created by a shrinking membership. That may mean postponing the day of decision until that shrinking membership has reduced the list of realistic options.

In the congregation that is on a plateau in size, the additional income may elevate the comfort level with the current level of member giving, and build dependency on that landlord role. Rather than focusing on improved stewardship, it may be easier to look for another tenant to help pay the bills. Financial subsidies, whether from the denominational treasury or an endowment fund, or rental income can pauperize what once was a healthy Christian fellowship.

Most serious of all, however, is that in the American economy, the natural, normal, and predictable arrangement between the landlord and tenant tends to drift from a cordial contract to an adversarial relationship. That immigrant congregation "takes over" space to which it is not entitled. The entrepreneurial woman who owns and operates the weekday child care center is also a highly skilled empire builder. Her empire expands far more rapidly than her interest in raising the annual rent. The five-year contract with that community organization called for an annual rental fee and did not include an escalator clause to allow for the impact of inflation or the cost of making physical improvements to the tenant's space. The expansion of the program of another tenant has resulted in longer hours, greater use of what were described in the contract as joint-use rooms, and higher utility bills than were anticipated. The agenda of the governing board is dominated by the demands of this relationship with tenants. Potential agenda concerns such as evangelism, worship, missions, music, and children are postponed until later. The urgent issues are relationships with the tenants and care of the real estate.

From this traveler's experience, the most productive scenarios for sharing physical facilities have been when that congregation has decided to relocate its meeting place, and the number-one tenant (or the only tenant) has signed a purchase agreement to acquire the real estate. That gives the seller time to look for or purchase that relocation property while being able to continue to worship for a year or two in its traditional meeting place. That landlord role is not one component of an institutional survival strategy, it is a means to an end in a larger ministry plan.

Is the Larger Parish a Promising Scenario?

Back in the 1950s one approach to staffing small rural congregations was a cooperative ministry often called the larger parish. The design called for several small congregations to share the leadership of one team. One larger parish, for example, included nine rural churches that varied in size from an average worship attendance of 15 to the largest average at 68. The combined average worship attendance for the nine was 360. The team consisted of two full-time pastors, the weekend services of a seminary student, a volunteer lay preacher who filled in when one of those three was ill or absent, plus a part-time parish secretary.

Back when that larger parish was created, farmers and ranchers constituted the majority in each of the nine congregations, and only 10 adults in that parish were college graduates. The 10 included one physician, the two ministers, a county agricultural agent, two high school teachers, the wife of a rancher, the wife of one of the two pastors, and the owner of a local drugstore.

The leaders in all nine of these congregations had their world-view shaped by the Great Depression of the 1930s and World War II. Their worldview assumed a scarcity of resources, geo-graphical isolation, a 3- to 5-mile radius as the natural service area for a Protestant congregation in rural America, and a special role by the ordained clergy that could not be filled by laypersons with relatively limited formal education or training.

The same sermon could be preached and be well received in any one of the nine churches. During most of the year, the three preachers rotated assignments. Each one led worship and preached in three congregations on the typical Sunday. By rotat-ing assignments, each of the three became well acquainted with the entire constituency. Each congregation heard each preacher at least 15 times during the course of the year. That reinforced the image the parish was being served by a team. Each became a familiar face and personality wherever he was assigned for that particular Sunday. The one exception was every three years brought a new seminary student to the weekend staff.

It was a great system and it worked. One reason it worked so well was the many points of commonality among the members of those nine congregations. Most of the adults were similar to their fellow members in terms of race, ancestry (all western European ancestry), language, level of formal education, ideology, social class, theological stance, marital status, income, culture, patriot-ism, standard of living, and expectations of what life owed them.

During the next half century, two of those small churches merged and one closed. In one of the remaining seven, the majority of adults today are retirees; in two the majority of adults are employed in the recreation and tourist industry. In one congre-gation the majority of the 43 adults are employed in a factory that opened in 1981, but only 5 of today's 43 members were born in this or an adjoining county, the others came with that factory and/or married a member. In the other three congregations the majority commute at least 20 miles each way five days a week to work in one of two nearby cities, one to the north and one to the west.

One consequence was the disintegration of that larger parish in 1987. One reason was the homogeneity among the constituents had been replaced by diversity and heterogeneity. A second reason was in four of the communities the increase in the number of residents had attracted new churches and raised the level of expectations among churchgoers. A third reason was the erosion of denominational loyalty that had been a powerful cohesive factor in the 1950s. A couple of paranoid members urged dissolving the arrangement because they were convinced a hidden goal was to close churches by encouraging mergers. One wise old-timer pointed out that the number-one reason for dissolving that cooperative ministry was that by 1987 most of the people who had created it had retired to the Sunbelt or were in nursing homes or cemeteries.

The moral of this story is this: the greater the degree of diversity within the constituencies and among congregational cultures, the more difficult it is to create and maintain cooperative ministries based largely on the geographical proximity of the meeting places and/or the denominational affiliation.

The larger parish was invented in an era when the constituency of a Christian congregation in America usually was defined in terms of denominational identities and geography rather than in terms of demographics and ideology. During the past half century, the differences among congregations, between the clergy and the laity, among the clergy and within denominational families have increased. Likewise the larger parish emerged before the arrival of the contemporary and greatly expanded affirmation of the ministry of the laity.

The merits of the potential value of the larger parish as a venture in interchurch cooperation should not be dismissed too lightly. If defined in nongeographical and interdenominational terms with a greatly expanded role for the laity and an open door to the use of modern technology, it may have its greatest days in the future.

Sharing a Pastor

The most common and the most influential of all approaches to the sharing of resources appears when two or more congregations share the ministerial services of the same pastor. Frequently the four most powerful variables in creating that sharing of resources are (1) none of the congregations can both afford and justify a full-time resident pastor, (2) the meeting places of the participating congregations are in relatively close geographical proximity, (3) the cooperating congregations have much in common in terms of size, the language used in the corporate worship of God, and theological stance, and (4) none of the congregations place a high priority on numerical growth.

Given those four motivations for sharing a pastor, this strategy also has much to commend it if the ultimate goal is the merger of two of those cooperating congregations. It also is an attractive option if each of the cooperating churches places a high value on "taking good care of our current members" and/or simply perpetuating the status quo.

On the other hand, this approach to sharing resources has several downsides. The obvious is what happens when a newcomer moves into that part of the world and, as a consequence of the choice of place of residence, could be attracted to and served by two or more of the congregations in that cooperative arrangement? If the newcomer concludes, "I am favorably impressed with that pastor!" does that minister encourage the newcomer to come to Church A or Church B?

Far more serious, what happens if that newcomer is repelled by the personality, theological stance, priorities, or preaching of that minister? That eliminates all participating congregations from the list of potential church homes for that newcomer.

The most subtle, and rarely discussed, potential downside is when the minister displays a relatively high level of skill and comfort with the distinctive culture of the small church. If numerical growth is not a priority, this is not a problem. The minister undergirds, affirms, and reinforces that distinctive small-church culture in each of the participating congregations, and everyone is happy.

This discussion helps to explain why over a 50-year period the majority of small churches utilizing this strategy experience a decrease in the number of constituents or dissolve or merge with another congregation. If, however, numerical growth is both possible and desired, it may be more productive to begin this conversation with a different question.

Who Will Be Our Partner?

Instead of beginning with the question "What can we share with others?" it may be more productive to ask "Who would make the best partners with our congregation?"

Do you believe that the best source of strength is to combine weakness with weakness? If so, you may want to partner with a relatively weak congregation. Or, do you believe it will be more beneficial for your congregation to partner with one of the missionary-type churches described in chapters 6 and 7? Do you believe the meeting places of your partners should be geographically close to yours? Or, is it more important they be theologically and ideologically close? Do you prefer intradenominational partnerships, or interdenominational partnerships? Or, is that not an issue since you prefer to cooperate with secular organizations serving the same core constituency as your church serves? That list could include hospitals, nearby employers with a daytime population paralleling your weekend constituents, retirees, tax-funded social service agencies, privately funded social service agencies, a public elementary school, a public high school, a private Christian school, out-of-town visitors to a recreation facility or a downtown convention center, job training centers, weekday child care programs, retirement centers, persons in jail or prison, residents of a mobile home park, a singles bar, service clubs, the manager of a nearby large apartment building, or the county fairgrounds down the street.

Do you want to build what can become long-term partnerships? Or, do you define your congregation as a "wounded bird" (see chapters 6 and 7) and prefer a short-term partnership with a missionary church that specializes in restoring wounded birds to health so they can fly by themselves?

Before answering, it may be useful to focus first on the best beginning questions.

What Are the Desired Outcomes?

What is the number-one priority or goal in your long-term ministry plan? How will you attempt to be responsive to what God is calling this congregation to be and to be doing during the next several years? What is at the heart of your call to ministry? Is it to maintain the Christian witness in this community that is symbolized by this meeting place? Is it to transmit the Christian faith to the children of today's members? Is it to become a fully self-expressing, self-propagating, self-governing, and self-financing congregation? Is it to enlist younger generations in full-time Christian service? Is it to raise money to support the goals of your denomination? Is it to merge with another nearby church? Is it to take good care of those Christians who prefer a small congregation that serves as a surrogate family?

Is it to evangelize and serve the unchurched residents of this neighborhood? Is it for a swift recovery of what is currently a wounded bird? Is it to make the transition from a neighborhood congregation into a regional church? (If so, the best partner may be what is now a self-identified mentoring church that has just completed that transition.) Is it to replace the old identity as an immigrant congregation with a new role? Is that number-one goal to provide your constituents with meaningful, memorable, and relevant sermons delivered by a superb communicator? (If so, a partnership with a missionary church that can provide a team of lay free agents, plus videotapes of sermons, described in chapter 6 may be the choice.) Or, is the number-one goal to replace the need for an ordained minister with indigenous leadership? (If so, chapters 6 and 7 offer possibilities.) Or, is the number-one goal to replace the old role as a generalist church with a clearly defined specialized niche? (See chapter 8.)

The point of that long paragraph is this. It may be helpful to reach an agreement on desired future outcomes before choosing a partner with whom your congregation will share resources. For those small churches that place a high priority on either significant numerical growth and/or a substantial redefinition of role and identity, the most productive option may not be to decide on how to share the services of a minister or how to share use of the real estate. A more creative and challenging option will be to build a relationship with that self-identified mentoring church that 10 or 15 years ago resembled what your congregation is today. Today that mentoring congregation resembles what you believe God is calling your church to be in the years ahead. Learn from those who have mastered "how to do church that way" in the 21st century.

Denominational agencies can render a valuable service by (1) identifying and encouraging these potential mentoring churches and resourcing them to be able to accept that role, and (2) encouraging smaller congregations to choose this road of building on strength. That is a far, far more difficult course of action than it first appears because it means planning from an assumption there is an abundance of resources and opportunities, rather than planning on the assumption there is a scarcity of resources.

CHAPTER TEN

THE ENDOWED CHURCH

Thousands of Protestant congregations in the United States have accumulated substantial amounts of wealth beyond what is required for current capital or operating expenses. This accumulated wealth may be referred to as "reserves," "a trust," "our endowment fund," or "The First Church Foundation." We are *not* referring to the assets in a building fund that have been earmarked for a specific capital expenditure, nor to the value of the land and buildings that constitute the current meeting place (and often were paid for by earlier generations of members). This discussion refers to capital assets—usually accumulated from memorial gifts, bequests, legacies, major gifts, plans for deferred giving, and investment income that are not yet designated for a specific purpose or recipient.

What is the new line of demarcation that divides these congregations into two categories? While a tiny number of congregations responded to this issue years ago, only recently has that line on a piece of paper grown into a high wall. One reason behind that line becoming a wall was that during the last decade or two of the 20th century, many churches found it relatively easy to attract the financial gifts that created these reserves. More than a few came unsolicited in the form of an unexpected large bequest. That affluent era also encouraged frugal leaders to actively seek the contributions that produced reserves, under one umbrella or another, equal to a few months to several years of operating expenses.

The Big Reason

The recent trend to build that wall, however, did not become a driving motivation until about 1998 or 1999. That motivation is called litigation. The national press eventually made it front-page news when several Roman Catholic dioceses in America became defendants in multimillion-dollar lawsuits. Those earlier judgments filed in the 1980s and 1990s rarely received much publicity. In 2001 and 2002, however, a new wave of investigative reporting made this into front-page news, and the subject of network television reporting. It suddenly became obvious that regional religious judicatories could be asked to pay millions of dollars in legal claims. While they never received the same amount of national publicity, dozens of Christian congregations also became the defendants in costly litigation.

One response was to build a legal wall around that accumulated wealth. That endowment fund, which had been controlled by the finance committee at Trinity Church, was transferred to a new separate legal entity incorporated as the Trinity Church Foundation, with its own self-perpetuating board of directors.

Concurrently, the threat posed by the doctrine of ascending liability motivated a variety of church-related homes, hospitals, colleges, camps, retreat centers, theological schools, newspapers, and resource ministries to construct a high legal wall that separated them from their denominational parents. That decision was reinforced by the conviction that as a completely separate legal entity they would have access to money that would not come their way if they retained their close church ties.

In congregational terms, the creation of this rising line of demarcation has caused congregational leaders in hundreds, perhaps thousands of churches, to ask themselves, "What would happen to our financial reserves if a plaintiff won a judgment against our church?"

The Three New Questions

Events of the past few years have placed three questions on the agenda of congregations of all sizes that previously had been content with a modest balance in the church's checking account at the end of the fiscal year.

1. Should we create an endowment fund? One argument in support is to accumulate financial reserves for that potential "rainy day." A second is, the annual income from investments could be used to meet rising expenditures. One argument against reserves, most of which will be in the form of bequests, is the difficulty in maintaining a healthy, live, and vital congregation that is living off the dead.

2. If we do decide to build up our financial reserves, how aggressive should we be in competing with all of the other religious, charitable, educational, and philanthropic organizations that already are asking our people to include them in that person's will or in making substantial financial contributions while still alive?[1] This has become a highly competitive facet of the American economy, and the passive usually end up holding an empty bag. Does your congregation actively encourage current members to remember their church in their wills? The estimated 10 percent that do usually receive in the form of bequests or cash contributions annual receipts that average out to the equivalent of 50 percent or more of the annual operating budget. The frequency and size of these gifts tend to be greatest in those congregations that display two or more of these characteristics: (a) an aging constituency; (b) in at least 48 weeks out of the year the Sunday morning bulletin includes a small box with the question, "Have you remembered your church in your will?" (approximately one-half of all American church members die before making out a will); (c) a once-a-year Sunday that includes a Sunday morning sermon on the Christian view of death plus afternoon workshops that are designed to help people deal with their own mortality, including how to prepare a checklist of answers to take to a lawyer for preparation of a will; (d) every member is provided with a brief but precise statement of the purpose of the endowment fund and celebrates what has been accomplished, thanks to that investment income; (e) the congregation rarely, if ever, "borrows" from the endowment fund to "balance the budget"; and (f) it carefully identifies the process for selecting the trustees of the endowment fund and their role.

3. If we do decide to launch an aggressive effort to receive these capital gifts, should they be held in the name of our congregation or be directed to and administered by a separate legal entity? A conservative guess is that at least one-fifth of those 160,000 American Protestant congregations averaging fewer than 75 at worship could accumulate reserves in an endowment or foundation of at least $500,000 by 2015, if the members agree this is a wise course of action.

Writing Your Own Rule Book

More than a century of experiences by American Protestant congregations provides clues to the potential consequences when a congregation does go down that road of encouraging one generation to finance future expressions of ministry through an endowment fund. These experiences suggest younger generations may bring a different perspective than was represented by the value system of those who contributed the original capital assets.

One creative writer described a foundation as a large body of money surrounded by people wanting to get their hands on those dollars. That creates three alternatives. One is to encourage internal quarreling over how those dollars may be spent. A second is to lament the fact that at least a few members will ask, "Why should I increase my giving when the church already has all that money?" A third alternative is to define as precisely as possible, either in the bylaws of the congregation or in the constitution of the foundation or trust, any restrictions on the allocations of those dollars. Frequently those restrictions or guidelines cover a dozen questions that can be included in your customized rule book:

1. How may those dollars be spent? For the benefit of that congregation? Or only for "outside" needs, causes, and institutions? Or both?
2. If for congregational needs, only the investment income? Or both investment income and accumulated assets? Can the capital assets be spent on "outside" causes?
3. May money, either from the investment income and/or the capital assets, be "loaned" to the congregation? If yes, at what interest rate? Must it be repaid with a repayment schedule? If that repayment schedule is not met, can additional "loans" be made?
4. May either investment income or capital assets be used to cover a shortfall or deficit in the operating budget of the church? Or to meet unbudgeted expenditures? If yes, only for unanticipated capital expenditures? Or for either unbudgeted operating or capital expenditures? (Permitting use of investment and/or capital assets for unbudgeted expenditures can encourage the finance committee to omit from the proposed budget probable future financial needs.)
5. When these grants are made to the congregation's treasury, may they be unrestricted? Or must they be matched (for example, dollar for dollar) by second-mile giving by the members?
6. May grants to the congregation's treasury be made only for launching new ministries (for example, to pay two-thirds of the costs the first year, and one-

third the second year), or may they be made to finance the continuation of ongoing ministries, such as an increase in the minister's compensation or to cover part of the annual utility bills?

7. May grants to the congregation be made to cover part or all of the costs for construction of a new building but not for renovation of the old meeting place? Or both?

8. Should grants to the congregation's treasury be restricted to expenditures for evangelism and missions? Or only for new ventures in missions and evangelism? Or only for matching grants?

9. Should there be a restriction on the allocation of funds from either the capital assets and/or investment income that grants may not be made for any purpose if and when the market value of the capital assets drop below a stated dollar amount?

10. Should the endowment fund or foundation take out a "key man" life insurance policy on the current minister, pay the annual premiums, and be the only beneficiary named in that policy?

11. What qualifies as approved investment of the capital assets? Corporate bonds? U.S. Treasury bonds? Insured certificates of deposit? Common stock? Preferred stocks? Real estate? May these capital assets be used to purchase land for the potential future relocation of the meeting place of this congregation? If so, is that a loan or a grant?

12. Should these bylaws or restrictions be designed to give future generations of leaders a high level of discretion in the allocation of these assets? Or to limit their discretion?

The most common model in American Protestantism does encourage dependency on the dead. That dependency relationship takes many forms. One of the worst is when the terminally ill, 81-year-old widow, who has included a generous bequest to the church in her will, returns to the hospital. The treasurer is seven weeks behind schedule in paying current operational expenses. Should the members of the finance committee meet and pray for that widow's recovery? Or pray for her death? Is a relatively high death rate among the current membership a symbol of concern or a cause for hope?

Lest there be any misunderstanding, this observer's position is to encourage congregations of all sizes to enter that contemporary competition for deferred giving. The American economy is well along in an unprecedented transfer of trillions of dollars of accumulated wealth from the generations born before 1950 to their children, grandchildren, other kinfolk, institutions of higher education, family foundations, community foundations, charitable causes, denominational foundations, governmental treasuries, private schools, hospitals, theological seminaries, museums, art galleries, congregations, parachurch organizations, public schools, and research centers. Perhaps your congregation's foundation should be added to that list? If your congregation decides to participate in this game, you can reduce the potential internal conflict by preparing your own customized rule book on how you will play the game.

CHAPTER ELEVEN

IS NUMERICAL GROWTH A GOAL?

I t was a hot, dry, and sunny late Wednesday afternoon in August 1933. A dairy farmer in Wisconsin had assembled all his livestock to hear an important announcement. His audience included 15 Holstein cows, 2 workhorses, a dozen pigs, 45 chickens, 2 mature cats, 1 kitten, and a collie.

"As you all know, our country is in a great depression," explained this 31-year-old farmer. "Prices for what we produce on this farm have never been this low. In order to meet our bills and pay our taxes, we must have a 10 percent increase in the amount of milk we produce every day. To achieve that goal, we must have the complete cooperation of everyone living on this farm."

As the farmer and his 6-year-old son walked away, the chickens clucked and said to one another, "What's this all about? We produce eggs for the farmer's wife to sell and meat for the family table. We don't have anything to do with milk production."

One horse shook his head in bewilderment and suggested to his cousin, "We would have been better off taking a late afternoon nap! We don't give milk. Why were we ordered to attend this meeting? Our job is to provide the power to plant and har-

vest the crops that produce the food the cows eat. Our big problem is the lack of rain. Instead of pestering us, the farmer and his
wife should go to prayer meeting later tonight and pray for rain.
That's their duty, not ours."

The oldest of the three elderly cows confided to her half-sister,
"Our future is not giving more milk, our future is hamburger."
One of the younger cows chewed her cud for a few minutes and
finally declared, "If he wants us to give more milk, we need better pasture and more grain in our diet. Exhortations are not an
adequate substitute for better food!"

The pigs held a caucus and quickly agreed, "Our number-one
responsibility is to lie in the sun and soak up the vitamin D we
don't get in the slop we're fed. Our number-two responsibility is
to convert skim milk, grain, and rye grass into pork. We do not
have any responsibility for producing more milk."

The kitten turned to his mother and meowed, "I thought this
was to be a memorial for my sister who was killed when one of the
horses stepped on her last week."

The collie explained, "My job is to get up early every morning,
seven days a week, bring the cows in from the pasture to be
milked, and go round them up again about this time every afternoon and herd them to the barn to be milked. I don't have anything to do with increasing milk production. If the farmer wants
more milk, he should buy a couple more cows."

Seven decades later, that farmer's grandson, Paul, who was not
even born until 1951, had graduated from college and seminary
and served two effective pastorates in numerically growing congregations averaging well over 300 at worship. A few months ago
he had been invited to join the program staff of one of the largest
regional judicatories in a mainline Protestant denomination. His
primary responsibility consists of two duties: to encourage every
congregation to place a high priority on evangelism and to help
congregations design and implement their own customized
church-growth strategies.

Recently he was explaining to a colleague in another regional
judicatory his early experiences. "When I came on board, I
decided I needed to learn in order to be an effective facilitator, so

I scheduled my first three visits with leaders from our three fastest-growing congregations. The first group explained to me that while others attributed their growth to the decision six years earlier to relocate the meeting place of this 96-year-old congregation from a functionally obsolete building on a tiny site at a well-concealed location, that was not the key variable. These folk insisted that was not the point. They declared the vote was really not on relocation. That congregational vote was a choice between trying to perpetuate their past versus creating a new future. The members voted 73 to 9 to create a new future. Relocation and the subsequent numerical growth were simply consequences of that decision.

"The leaders in the second of these congregations explained to me their numerical growth also was the consequence of a fork-in-the-road decision," continued this farmer's grandson. "That congregation had been founded in 1949 as a neighborhood church. A member of the sponsoring church had given the new mission a 5-acre parcel of land near the intersection of a state highway and a county road. After 20 years they were averaging nearly 200 at worship and welcomed everyone to come and worship with them in this neighborhood church. By 1989, however, their attendance had dropped to an average of 113, and that is when they made their critical fork-in-the-road decision. Instead of attempting to welcome and please everyone, they decided to focus on what they defined as a neglected constituency. Most of their competitors were trying to attract young families with children at home. They decided not to compete in that market. Instead, thanks partly to the arrival of a new pastor born back before this congregation had been founded, they decided to focus on mature adults. A dozen years ago they began offering a high-quality traditional worship service with a robed chancel choir and outstanding biblical preaching. Currently they offer two worship services on Sunday morning, with adult classes meeting at both hours. A noon luncheon is served 50 Sundays a year. They also offer a ten o'clock Wednesday morning combination worship service and Bible study that concludes with lunch. Most of the 60 or so attendees are seniors living alone. About 20 times a year the

Greyhound-type bus they own is scheduled for a major trip that lasts anywhere from two to 10 days. They claim that bus is the most productive component of their church-growth strategy. Members invite friends, neighbors, and relatives to go on these trips. When they return, these strangers come back with a new set of close friends. Last year their combined average church attendance for those two services was nearly 350. Their paid staff now includes the pastor, who helped initiate this, a semiretired social worker, a part-time parish nurse, a gregarious retired minister who runs the bus ministry and preaches a half dozen times a year, and a part-time retired elementary school principal who runs the adult learning ministries.

"Our third success story goes back to a small open-country rural church founded in 1873 that averaged between 20 and 45 at worship for well over a century," continued Paul. "In 1982 a widow left the church $100,000. Instead of starting an endowment fund, they decided to replace the minister they shared with a somewhat larger congregation in a nearby town with a full-time resident pastor. They had been paying one-third of the total compensation of their part-time minister. Thanks to the legacy, they were able to guarantee the new minister a market-rate compensation package, including a housing allowance for at least three years."

"What happened?" interrupted the impatient colleague.

"Three years after the arrival of the new pastor, the average worship attendance had jumped from 38 to 129, but about a fourth of the members had dropped out because they were unhappy with all the changes that were being made. A year or so later a farmer who was a fifth-generation member gave the congregation 30 acres of land on the west side of the church's property. Since then, they have completed three building programs and accepted a role as a large regional church serving people from about a 20-mile radius, and their church attendance now is approaching a thousand every weekend."

"The thread I see running through all three of those stories is discontinuity with the past," reflected the colleague. "Is that how you see it?"

"Yes and no," was the instant reply. "Let me explain that by telling you about three of my more recent experiences. The first was with a small rural congregation that averages about 35 to 40 at worship. When I explained that the purpose of our meeting was to help them design a church-growth strategy, they explained they already had one. They told me their responsibility was to transmit the Christian faith to the children of their members. When the children subsequently leave that community to go away to school or in search of a city job, they will be prepared to join a church of our denomination near their new place of residence. When I suggested they also could be evangelizing the unchurched, they replied they did not have the resources to do both, and they had chosen to evangelize their own children rather than unchurched adults.

"Later on I visited a midsized congregation in a growing suburban community where a recent survey by a seminary professor had pointed out that one-third of the adult residents had no active current church relationship," continued Paul. "When I offered to help them design a customized church-growth strategy, they pointed out that many years earlier a beloved and influential pastor had persuaded them that the first 20 cents out of every dollar in the offering plate should be sent to denominational headquarters to help finance worldwide efforts in missions and evangelism, they insisted they had their priorities well in hand and that it was somewhat presumptuous of me to come in and attempt to persuade them to abandon the teachings of that beloved pastor, who, incidentally, had died nine years earlier. One lesson I learned was that being dead doesn't mean you're gone!"

"Both of those reinforce my point that a strategy for church growth really requires affirmation of discontinuity with the past," insisted the colleague.

"I won't argue with you on that, but I believe the issue is a bit more complicated," declared Paul. "Two weeks ago I met with the leaders of one of our inner-city congregations. North Church was founded in 1891 by our downtown First Church. It peaked in attendance in the early 1950s with an average worship attendance of nearly 400. That marked the end of an era when this church served an upper-middle and upper-class constituency. By the mid-1950s most of them were moving to better and newer housing to the west and north. A shrinking number came back to church. Several remembered the church in their wills. Today, North Church averages 97 at worship, and it has an endowment fund valued at over $2 million. Nearly half of their $218,000 annual budget is financed with investment income. The median age of the confirmed membership is 68 years. Two years ago they spent nearly $300,000 to remodel the masonry building constructed in 1927 following a fire that completely destroyed the original wooden frame church. Slightly over half of that $300,000 came from two bequests, and the rest came from the members in a one-year capital funds campaign. The staff includes a full-time 58-year-old minister who is an average preacher but a superb loving shepherd, a part-time church nurse, a full-time receptionist-secretary, a couple who serve as custodians, and a semiretired minister of pastoral care. I left there convinced the level of discontent with the status quo among the members was as close to zero as in any congregation I have ever visited. When I introduced the subject of church growth, they explained that is one of their priorities. Every year they send $10,000 to a new mission our denomination planted six years ago in the next county, and $5,000 to a sister church in Slovakia."

"What's your point?" challenged the colleague.

"Those and several similar experiences have convinced me I was misled when I was told my job would be to help congregations design a customized church-growth strategy," reflected Paul. "One barrier, as you have pointed out, is that the real issue is not evangelism, it is an openness to discontinuity with the past. A second barrier, however, is many, perhaps even most of our churches, do not see church growth as their responsibility. That is someone else's burden, not theirs. An ancient bit of wisdom in the field of adult education is, you cannot teach an adult anything that adult does not want to learn."

"Add teenagers to that list," corrected the colleague, who recently survived rearing two teenagers.

"My point is that it is ridiculous to suggest that every congregation should be challenged to enlist 5 or 10 or 50 new members or to grow by 10 percent annually. I agree with the people who created the position I now hold," explained Paul. "We have had enough failures with the one-size-fits-all formulas on how to do church growth. One of the primary reasons I left the pastorate for this job is that I was attracted by the proposal that every congregation needed to design its own customized ministry plan. I am in complete agreement with that concept. What has raised my frustration level is I had not anticipated that a big barrier would be a refusal by congregational leaders to accept that as a given in defining the ministry of their church. I came expecting to be a specialist in church growth. That's what my job description calls for me to be and do. The real need, however, is for skills in how an outsider can introduce change in an organization. As a pastor, I learned that's easier for an insider than for an outsider."

"Maybe you should identify your role as an interventionist rather than as a church-growth specialist?" questioned the colleague.[1]

"That's exactly my first point," was Paul's quick response. "My second point, however, is how do you persuade the pigs and the horses they have a responsibility to help increase milk production on a dairy farm?"

The following Saturday, Paul took another step up the learning curve as he spent the day meeting with the leaders of a village church founded in 1889. The last full-time resident pastor left in 1953. For the past half century it has been served by a series of ministers who concurrently served a similar size congregation in a small city 7 miles to the north and it provides the pastor with a church-owned house. Both congregations have been averaging between 50 and 60 at worship for at least three decades. During these 50 years of sharing a pastor, 11 different ministers have served this cooperative venture. The longest tenure was seven years, and the shortest two years.

After nearly two hours of what Paul felt to be a frustration-producing discussion, he responded to one negative comment with this challenge, "If I understand you correctly, you're telling me you would like to see this congregation grow as long as that doesn't require bringing in more people."

"No, you don't understand what we've been trying to explain to you," replied Dave, a fourth-generation member who teaches social studies in one of the two local public junior high schools. "Back in 1948 my grandfather was in the last graduating class of the high school in this village. The state had changed the formula for financial aid to public schools in 1943. The new formula made it financially attractive to consolidate the public schools and nearly impossible to continue the small four-year public high school with approximately 100 students. Fifty-five years later, this school district includes one three-year high school with 700 students, two junior highs with a combined enrollment of nearly 800, and five elementary schools with a combined K-6 enrollment of close to 1,700. Our old high school, which has been remodeled into a community center, is a half mile west of this church. The new consolidated public high school is 9 miles north of here."

"That's a pattern we see all across this state," commented Paul. "I checked the census data before coming here, and between 1960 and 2000 this end of the county has nearly doubled in population, but your church is about the same size it was 50 years ago. It seems to me only logical to expect this congregation should have doubled in size rather than remained on a plateau. This is why I asked, do you want to design a strategy to attract some of the newcomers to this community? Your description of what has happened here is simply one more illustration of the fact that we are moving from a culture filled with small institutions to an economy dominated by big institutions. Do you see a bright future for small churches such as this one?"

"That greatly oversimplifies the issue," replied Dave, who represented one of three family trees that accounted for well over half of the current membership of this small-town church. "The real question is do we want to pay the price of doubling or tripling or quadrupling in size? Most of us in this room know the consequences of school consolidation. We swapped a small four-year public high school on the edge of town for access to a large three-year high school 9 miles away. That old building also housed our two-room eight grade elementary school. That has been replaced by a new and larger elementary school in a village 6 miles east of here. All of our children are transported to that school by bus. For several generations our school was the number-one center of community life here. We traded that for what we were told would be superior educational opportunities for our children and youth. Our hardware store closed about 20 years later. A few years after that, one of the two general stores closed when the owners retired and no one wanted to buy it. Seven years ago the other store, which had been turned into a combination grocery and convenience store, closed when a big national supermarket opened across the street from the high school north of here. We're now left with a tavern, three churches, one gasoline station, and the post office—and the government is threatening to close the post office. Ten years ago the Presbyterian church down the street decided to merge with the Presbyterian church in the village where the elementary school is located."

"Parallels to your story can be found in scores of other small towns all across our state," interrupted Paul. "On the way over here, along the county road leading into town, however, I counted about two dozen new houses that look like they were constructed within the past several years. Do you want to reach and serve some of those families?"

"If you check every road and street within 5 miles of here, I expect you would find at least 60 of those houses," explained Dave. "They've been built by or for families that don't mind a long commute to work. They want to combine a city paycheck with country living. My wife and I built one of them 12 years ago. We decided we wanted to continue to live close to my parents and my brother and his wife. My daily commute to the junior high where I teach is only 7 miles; hers is 12 each way. Bob and Michelle, who are sitting right behind me, also live in one of those new houses you saw. Bob travels for a living, and there is a good regional airport 30 miles south of here. He drives to that about 40 times a year and makes a good living. Neither one of them is a native of this state, but they decided this would be a great place to rear their three children. They joined our church about four years ago, and today they're among the pillars of this congregation."

"So you are able to welcome newcomers," affirmed the denominational staffer. "My question is, do you want to welcome more of them?"

"Let me add a word here," interrupted Michelle. "As Dave told you, Bob and I are new here. We moved here four years ago. The church we left behind averaged well over 600 at worship. After nine years there, at least half of the members still were complete strangers to us. We picked this church because we didn't want the anonymity and complexity of a big congregation. We traded a church with an extensive program for one that serves as a surrogate family for us. Here we know every member. More important, most of our closest friends come from among the members here. Dave and his wife are two of them. We're part of a Bible study and prayer group that meets every Tuesday evening. There are five couples in that group. Six of the 10 of us were reared in this church, while four of us are relatively new. That group means more to Bob and me than any ministry in the church we left when we moved here."

"Well, let me put it another way," persisted Paul. "I believe that evangelism should be a central component of the life and ministry of every church. Do you agree?"

"That depends on your definition of the word *church*," challenged Dave. "This congregation is affiliated with a denomination that uses the word *church* as the last word in its name. I agree that means it should be an evangelistic body. That does not mean, however, that every congregation has to do what the denomination does. For example, the last three times I have talked with you, I've urged that our denomination should plant a new mission near the high school north of here. This congregation can't do that. Our denomination can. We'll be glad to schedule a special financial appeal to help pay for it, but we can't plant a new mission all by ourselves. That doesn't mean we don't have a right to exist!"

"We've been talking about a new mission north of here," confirmed Paul, "but that's not the agenda for this meeting. The question here is, do you want to see this church grow or remain on a plateau in size?"

"I agree with Dave that is not the issue," declared Bob. "The central question is trade-offs. As Dave pointed out earlier, this community already has traded off a huge chunk of the cohesive forces that held it together in order to be a part of a consolidated school district. That's history. We cannot reverse that, but we can learn from history. I'm reasonably sure that if we abandoned the property where this congregation has been worshiping since before 1900 and constructed new facilities on a 5-acre site out in the country, we could be averaging at least a hundred at worship within five years. The trade-offs are more than some of us want to make. We now are one of the few remaining cohesive ties left in this small town. We would swap intimacy for anonymity. We would trade decision making by consensus for a representative system of governance. Instead of being happy with the minister who serves as our part-time pastor, we would need our own full-time minister. Instead of being at the center of life for many of our people, we would become one of several organizations competing for their loyalty, their time, and their money."

"That's not why we moved out here," added Michelle. "I also resent the suggestion we are too small to be viable. Last year we averaged 53 at worship. Recently I read in a book that there are at least 90,000 Protestant churches in America that average fewer than we do at worship, compared to only 15,000 that average more than 500 at worship. We're not the only ones who prefer a small church!"

"What you say is true, and it also reflects the distribution of churches by size in this denomination," agreed Paul, "but you need to add one more pair of numbers to this analysis. In our denomination the smallest 70 percent of our congregations account for only 30 percent of our total worship attendance on the typical weekend. The majority of churchgoers apparently prefer large congregations."

"That may be true, but that's simply one more example of a theme that has run through American history for more than 200 years," added Dave. "That is the conflict between majority rule and minority rights. I have no problem with the fact that the majority prefer large churches as long as they accept the fact that some of us prefer small congregations."

The Real Issue

This conversation introduces one of the most divisive issues on the agenda of the typical small and midsized congregation organized before 1980. Frequently that issue is condensed into a five-word question: "Do you want to grow?" Sometimes it is presented wrapped in a blanket of guilt-inducing rhetoric. A better statement of the issue is, "Are you willing to initiate the changes and accept the trade-offs that will be required to reach, attract, welcome, serve, assimilate, and challenge larger numbers of people, most of whom have no previous tie to this congregation?"

That pair of questions ranks right up there beside the two addressed to the adult who is 40 pounds overweight. One is, "Would you like to reduce your weight?" The second is, "Are you willing to make major changes in your diet and increase your exercise in order to lose weight?" The first evokes an easy, "Yes." At best, the second raises a response of "Tell me more."

Addition or Multiplication?

The response of "Tell me more" introduces a big fork-in-the-road to tomorrow. Do you want to grow by adding more people? For example, in the average year that congregation averaging 53 at worship may lose three or four people who die, drop out, switch to another church, or move away. Will they be replaced by adding two or three or four or five people? If every year an average of four subtractions are replaced by an average of five additions, this congregation could double in size in only 50 years. A persistent, continuing, and reasonably high-quality invitational church-growth strategy could produce a moderate rate of numerical growth in most small churches. That approach also probably would produce an acceptable rate of change. The big reservation is, a substantial increase in population probably will raise the level of competition among the churches for potential future constituents and make it more difficult to replace everyone who departs. One alternative could be to choose a multiplication approach to growth. This could call for replacing that part-time pastor with a full-time resident minister, while concurrently replacing the consensus model for decision making with a pastor-led model.

A few months after arriving, that new pastor might add a Saturday evening worship service to the schedule, and a year or two later expand the Sunday morning schedule to two worship experiences. That would transform this from a congregation of 27 households into a congregation of congregations. Experience suggests that by the end of five years, five to eight of those current 27 households would have left feeling they had been betrayed by the new pastor. After all, they had chosen that congregation because they preferred a small church. Five years after the arrival of the new pastor, the combined attendance of those three weekend worship experiences would be averaging 120 to 135. Instead of gradually adding individuals, this strategy calls for multiplying the number of worshiping communities meeting under the same roof. The price tags include an increase in the anonymity, a rise in the level of complexity, the professionalization of the leadership, a reduction in the control of the laity, and replacing the denominational affiliation as the heart of congregational identity with the pastor as the center of the community image. A more moderate approach could be to affiliate with a large church of that denomination located in that city 30 miles to the south and become "the north campus" of that ministry center. (See chapters 6 and 7.)

Another multiplication model could be to replace the old image as a stable institution in a sea of change and decide to become a new church in new facilities at a new location. The invitation would be, "Come help pioneer the creation of a new church for a new day." A modest goal would be an average worship attendance of 135 by the end of the fifth year. This scenario requires replacing the comfort of continuity with the past with the stresses of discontinuity. That usually requires the leadership of a pastor with patience and far above average skills as an agent of planned change initiated from within the organization.

In summary, rather than dream about numerical growth, if that is the goal, ask, "Should we plan to grow slowly by addition or more rapidly by multiplication?" That answer should be consistent with the response to the question, "How much discontinuity with the past are we prepared to accept?" As was pointed out in the middle of chapter 3, this would require replacing the central organizing principles that have held this congregation together for so long with a new set of organizing principles.

Should those congregations that reject suggestions that they design and implement a church-growth strategy that will enable them to double or triple their size be dismissed as obsolete or irrelevant or not fully Christian? First of all, as the critics of the bean counters agree, numbers are one way, but not the only way, to evaluate a religious movement or institution.[2] Second, fewer than one-fifth of the creatures on that farm owned by Paul Baker's grandfather back in the 1930s actually produced the milk that paid the bills and the taxes, but it was a good place for the rearing of Paul's father. It also was a place where the chickens, pigs, horses, and cats felt they could justify their existence.

CHAPTER TWELVE

WHAT ABOUT THOSE NINTH-GRADERS?

For decades public school administrators have been grappling with what to do with ninth-graders. One assumption is they are too old, too big, and too mature to be mixed in with seventh- and eighth-graders, and therefore should be enrolled in a four-year high school. A second strategy is based on the assumption they are too young and too immature to be in a four-year high school, and they will thrive in a junior high school consisting of seventh-, eighth-, and ninth-graders.

Which is the better pedagogical environment? One in which ninth-graders are identified as "the big kids," or one in which they are identified as "the little kids"?

The radical solution has been to create a one-year middle school with the enrollment limited to ninth-graders only. This issue is complicated by the fact that none of these three alternatives is appropriate for every ninth-grader. The research suggests that a majority of ninth-graders will do well in a four-year, single-

143

sex, and highly structured academic high school that also mixes students across grade levels in a variety of extracurricular activities with a total enrollment under 500. Other ninth-graders are more comfortable in a junior high school for grades 7 through 9, while the single grade school for ninth-graders excels in training students how to make the transition from one environment to another twice in 13 or 14 months. A substantial number, but far less than 100 percent, of ninth-graders flourish in the co-ed, four-year high school with a total enrollment in the 1,500 to 3,000 range. This is an especially productive environment for those who place a high value on public high schools serving as farm clubs for university athletic teams. A growing number of ninth-graders are choosing the home-schooling alternative. The high school or junior high that is affiliated with the Reserve Officers' Training Corps usually has a waiting list of teenagers wanting to enroll. Advocates of parental choice contend that the tax-funded charter school provides the best pedagogical environment for ninth-graders. Many parents prefer a tuition-financed private secular school for their ninth-graders. Others choose an avowedly Christian school for theirs.

The moral of this introduction is that the producer-driven model of planning tends to offer far fewer options than the consumer-driven model. Which model should be used in planning for the education of ninth-graders? Which model should be used in planning for the future of all those small American Protestant congregations? In other words, no one design can provide the ideal pedagogical environment for all ninth-graders. Likewise, no one strategy or ministry plan is appropriate for every one of the 25,000 American Protestant congregations averaging between 101 and 125 at worship.

The parallel in American Protestantism, as was suggested earlier in the first chapter, is most of those 25,000 congregations averaging 101 to 125 tend to be too large to be labeled "small churches." After all, an average worship attendance of more than 100 means that congregation is larger than 62 percent of all PCUSA congregations, larger than 59 percent of all Episcopal parishes, larger than 72 percent of all United Methodist congregations, and larger than 60 percent of all Southern Baptist churches. If you are taller than three out of five, the only place the nickname "Shorty" is appropriate is on the basketball court.

Unlike public school administrators, the leaders in congregations in this size category have more than three courses of action open to them. How many? That depends on two crucial variables.

First, do the leaders believe they are planning from a base of strength, or from a base of weakness? Are we dealing with a low ceiling on what can happen, or a high ceiling? The stronger the conviction and the more widely shared the conviction that the ceiling on the future is relatively high, the longer that list of alternative courses of action.

The second variable is the local context. That includes the community setting, the location, quality, and size of the congregation's meeting place, relevant demographic patterns, plus the role and identity of the other Christian churches serving that community.

What are the possible courses of action for the approximately 25,000 Protestant congregations in this size bracket? If it was founded to serve as a neighborhood church for nearby residents, if it has adequate meeting rooms and owns at least 75 to 100 off-street parking spaces, one alternative is to carve out a distinctive niche serving a regional constituency. The better the quality of the buildings, the larger the site; and the greater the visibility and accessibility, the better the chances of becoming a midsized regional church.

For many more, the most attractive option may be to lift the size to that comfortable level of 125 to 140 at worship. Literally, thousands of American Protestant congregations identify that as the ideal comfort zone. They are able to minimize the anonymity and complexity that is a characteristic of larger congregations, but are able to mobilize the resources (volunteers, money, staff, real estate) required to respond to the personal and religious needs of many people.[1]

If this congregation is meeting in a functionally obsolete building on an inadequate site at what no longer is an attractive location, the most prudent course of action may be to relocate the meeting place as part of a larger strategy to create a new future.

Should we relocate? Or, should we continue to meet at this sacred place? A growing number of congregations are answering that pair of questions with these words: "Yes. We will become a two-site church." A second meeting place (sometimes in a strip shopping center) is purchased or leased, and the Sunday morning schedule calls for the minister to be at the early service at one site, and at the other location for the second service. Obviously, this option requires a cooperative pastor who does not intend to depart for at least several more years.

A fourth option is described in chapter 8: carve out a distinctive niche that is defined in terms of ministry rather than geography. Another alternative is described in chapter 6: accept the role of the missionary church that identifies, enlists, challenges, empowers, equips, places, and supports the teams of free agents who provide leadership to small congregations.

Perhaps the easiest alternative is to affiliate with one of those very large churches that has become a multiple-campus ministry. (See chapter 7.) Ask to become the north (or west or south or east) campus and enjoy the benefits of being able to relate to all the ministries and opportunities of the megachurch, but retain the intimacy, fellowship, and relative simplicity of church life that is a characteristic of the congregation averaging 100, more or less, at worship. For some, the number-one price tag on this option is henceforth we relate to "our staff" rather than to "our pastor."

At least a couple thousand congregations in this size bracket may want to ensure their future by creating a substantial endowment fund. A few of the pluses and minuses of that option are discussed in chapter 10.

That is far from an exhaustive list! It is offered here for two reasons. One is to stimulate creative thinking. The other, and more important, is to emphasize popular options that should not be on the list of alternatives for most of the congregations in this size bracket.

Seven Popular Scenarios

A brief word should be offered here about seven popular options that have not been included on this first list. The first two were omitted because they tend to be extremely difficult to accomplish. The remaining five tend to fall between being counterproductive and subversive.

By far the most difficult to implement of all these options is to find a new pastor who preaches persuasive, inspiring, and meaningful sermons at the certainty end of that spectrum described earlier in chapter 3. It also helps to implement this scenario if that minister also brings a magnetic personality; is a visionary leader who finds it easy to enlist enthusiastic support for that vision of a new tomorrow; possesses superb administrative talents; is a creative fundraiser; excels as a teacher; is a remarkably productive worker; serves as an attractive role model for teenagers; calls everyone, regardless of age, correctly by name, including parakeets, cats, dogs, and distant kinfolk of the members; excels at funerals; and is married to a spouse who has inherited substantial wealth. The demand for these ministers exceeds the supply by at least a 1,000-to-1 ratio. Even the ministers who pull off middle-sized miracles are in short supply.

Another difficult, but much easier, alternative is for the congregation that has fluctuated in size between 50 and 135 at worship for the past 40 years or more to grow into a congregation averaging 350 or more at worship. The success stories under this umbrella usually involve the relocation of the meeting place, a transformation of the congregational culture, the arrival of a new minister who serves that congregation for at least 15 to 20 years, and the disappearance of a dozen or more long-tenured pillars who display zero interest in being part of a big church. "One of the reasons we joined this congregation 20 years ago was we didn't want to be part of a big church." They have been betrayed by (1) that new minister, and (2) their longtime friends who are enthusiastic supporters of this new era.

The most subversive but highly popular scenario is a response to the problem of "How do we pay our bills?" A difficult-to-implement response is to improve the level of stewardship. A more attractive option is to accept a landlord role and "rent out our building." The price tags on this option are identified in chapter 9. A fourth popular option, to share a pastor with one or more other congregations, also is evaluated in chapter 9.

The fifth option, which continues to be popular with many small churches but is being removed from the list by an increasing number of denominations, is the long-term financial subsidy. This often was justified in the past when denominational treasuries were fuller by one of three explanations: "We must continue a Christian witness by our denomination in that community." "This congregation has been a loyal supporter of our denominational goals for years. They have experienced some recent misfortunes, and we have an obligation to help them get back on their feet." "Several years ago we were convinced this was the place to plant a new mission to reach and serve that constituency. We had hoped that it would have become a fully self-expressing, self-governing, self-propagating, and self-financing congregation by now, but that hasn't happened. We continue to believe in that vision, and so we will continue the financial subsidy." One reason to continue that subsidy is to demonstrate that long-term financial subsidies are more likely to nurture dependency rather than to spark effective evangelistic efforts.

A sixth popular dream for these congregations is illustrated by this comment: "Last month it was announced that 500 new dwelling units will be constructed a half mile west of our church. If we can attract only one-tenth of those families, that would double our size."

Real-life experiences suggest that these newcomers—whether they be in the central city, an aging suburb, or an exurbia—are more likely to prefer to help pioneer the new rather than to join in perpetuating the old. Experience also suggests that fewer than 100 percent of those long-established small churches will be able to attract, welcome, assimilate, and earn the loyalty of even 5 percent of that flood of newcomers.

A seventh alternative that is popular in several denominations is illustrated by this comment: "We know we cannot afford a full-time pastor, but we own a nice parsonage. We believe God has called us to provide a two- or three-year apprenticeship to married seminary students who need a place to live and are satisfied with a modest salary. They combine their seminary work with serving as our pastor. Their seminary classes enrich their ministry here, and their work with us enriches their classroom learning experiences. This creates a win-win-win situation for us, for the student, and for the seminary. Several of our former ministers have gone on to outstanding careers as parish pastors."

This arrangement raises three questions. First, who is the number-one client? Second, is this a good way to guarantee these small churches will be served by a passing parade of short pastorates? Third, is discontinuity in ministerial leadership the best way to create attractive, vital, vigorous, mission-driven, and spiritually healthy congregations?

Two Rarely Traveled Roads

If numerical growth is the top priority in a congregation currently averaging 90 to 125 at worship that also is seeking a full-time resident pastor, one option is to become a high-commitment church that projects very high expectations of anyone seeking to become a full member, or to continue as a full member.

This strategy is easiest to implement in the new mission. The second easiest is in the congregation that has (1) decided to relocate the meeting place as one component of a new strategy to reach a larger constituency, (2) agreed to redefine its identity and self-image into becoming a high-commitment church, and (3) attracted the leadership of a pastor born after 1965 who is both willing and able to lead in the achievement of those first two goals. This usually means that pastor fully understands the pluses and minuses of this transformation in identity and role. It also means that minister is a far above average preacher or is comfortable utilizing videotapes of preachers who excel in both content and delivery. The reason a relatively young age is mentioned is this scenario usually requires a pastorate in excess of two decades.

Among the common outcomes of this strategy are (1) the departure of perhaps 10 to 20 percent of the longtime members who oppose relocation of the meeting place, (2) the departure of another 10 to 20 percent who prefer to be part of a low-commitment church, and (3) a doubling of the average worship attendance every five to seven years beginning with the second or third year of that new identity. In one congregation founded in 1900 that relocated in 1979, the average worship attendance plunged from 118 to 81, doubled over the next five years to 160, doubled again during the next six years to 335, and doubled again after another seven years to over 700. One explanation was much better physical facilities on an 18-acre site at a highly attractive location. A second was the continuity of what had become a 20-year pastorate. A third was the creation of an excellent program staff team. A fourth, and perhaps the most crucial, was replacing the old rulebook with a new one.

That old rule book (the actual operational policies) called for this congregation to welcome everyone; to operate with a low threshold into membership that required attendance at three one-hour prospective new member classes; to not remove any person's name from the membership roster unless the person had been absent from worship for at least 52 consecutive weekends and also had failed to make any financial contribution for at least one year; to assume that at least one-third of the members would not be worshiping there on the typical weekend (that was reflected in both the seating capacity for worship and the availability of conveniently located parking); to expect the pastor would "move on" after four to seven years; to assume that the existing network of classes, circles, groups, choirs, organizations, and social networks would be able to assimilate all newcomers; and to define missions as sending money to other organizations to "do missions on our behalf."

That new minister had brought together an alliance of leaders who created a new set of operational policies. The relocation planning was based on the assumption that on at least 48 weekends a year, weekend worship attendance would exceed the membership and the new parking lot would accommodate two motor vehicles for every three worshipers on the typical weekend. This new rule book also assumed that "we welcome everyone who wants to come and worship God with a Trinitarian congregation," but the threshold into membership was raised. This new rule book calls for 42 weeks of two-hour classes for anyone seeking to become a member. ("We don't want anyone asking to join unless they fully understand who we are, what we believe, what we teach, and what we do.") Admission to those classes is restricted to persons who, during the past year, have (1) been a regular participant in weekend worship here, (2) become an active participant in a small group such as an adult Sunday school class or choir or weeknight Bible study group or missional task force or mutual support group, (3) committed themselves to tithing and returning at least one-half of that tithe to the Lord by way of this congregation's treasury, and (4) begun the process of identifying their spiritual gifts and how those gifts could be used in ministry.

Everyone who was a member was "grandfathered" into full membership a month before the move to their new meeting place, but more than 20 absences from weekly worship during any 12-month period opened the door to the question, "Do you want to continue to be a member here?"

One consequence was scores of people worshiped with this congregation for a year or more before inquiring about membership. A second consequence was the creation of a new category. These are the "constituents" who want to be a part of this worshiping community but are not willing to climb that high threshold into membership. A third consequence was highlighted at the celebration of the 20th anniversary of that move to the new address. At that celebration the average attendance for the three weekend services was 708, and the full members numbered 314. A fourth consequence was 73 percent of the dollar receipts for the previous year came from 28 percent of the contributing households. A fifth consequence, since that new rulebook

151

declared only full members may serve as teachers or hold policy-making volunteer leadership positions, was the creation in year 14 at the new address of a 30-hour per week staff position for a laywoman who had two responsibilities: (1) the overseeing of that network of volunteers, and (2) the assimilation of newcomers. A sixth consequence was that in the typical recent year the number of newcomers (both new constituents and new names on the membership roster), averaged approximately 160, and the number of departures numbered approximately 130. High-commitment churches usually experience a relatively high turnover in the total constituency. Part of that can be explained by the fact that high-commitment churches tend to attract a disproportionately large number of younger adults.

WARNING! This scenario requires the long tenure of a pastor who is a strong advocate of high-commitment congregations. Those small congregations in which the local tradition calls for welcoming a new minister every three to seven years probably will find it extremely difficult to adopt this scenario.

The Lay Team

The second of these two rarely traveled roads is a variation on chapter 6 and also assumes the time has come to empower the laity. Instead of searching for a full-time and fully credentialed seminary graduate to come and serve as the pastor of the congregation averaging around 100 at worship, the leaders of that congregation take the initiative to go down another road. Instead of looking for a generalist who excels in all areas of ministry, this process begins by dividing those responsibilities into several components.

The desired outcome of that process is to build a team of part-time specialists at a modest dollar cost. That team could be composed of these 10 lay free agents: That woman who retired recently after three decades as an administrator in a nonprofit organization serves as the church business administrator. A gifted amateur vocalist assembles, rehearses, and leads a worship team of five volunteers. A 16-year-old high schooler comes on board as the volunteer media expert. A retired teacher serves as the worship leader and introduces the Sunday morning message delivered by way of videotape by one or more top-quality preachers. A retired nurse serves as the leader of a team of five volunteers who have completed Stephen Ministries training; together they fill the need for pastoral care. A widowed adult completes the 10 two-hour sessions designed to prepare a layperson to officiate at funerals. A teacher at the local community college agrees to design and lead a six-evening course once a year for Sunday school teachers. A mother of three volunteers to organize and direct a children's choir. A self-identified lifelong learner volunteers to watch that videotape of the Sunday morning message a few days early and prepares and leads a discussion of that message with the adult class (ages 14 and over) that gathers every Sunday after worship. The most gregarious and extroverted member of the congregation agrees to ignore longtime friends every Sunday morning in order to greet and welcome newcomers.

Five or six of the 10 members of that leadership team are enlisted from within the current membership, and four or five are "borrowed" from self-identified missionary churches.

Outsiders can help facilitate the efforts required to implement change. A second reason is to enrich the talent pool. The total annual dollar cost, including reimbursement of expenses and a few modest stipends for the heaviest responsibilities, probably will be between $8,000 and $25,000.

To go back to the theme of chapter 5, which road is most likely to produce the desired outcomes? The search for a superstar? Or, building a talented team by challenging gifted free agents?

SHOULD WE MERGE?

The reason I called to make an appointment to come by and see you was that I've been told this congregation is the product of a highly successful merger. I want to learn about what you've done and how you've done it." That was my introductory statement as I shook hands with the 45-year-old pastor.

"I'll be glad to try to answer your questions," came the gracious reply, "but you need to understand this was not a merger. It was a union of three small churches. One was a congregation founded in 1873 as a German immigrant church. It peaked in size in the 1930s when it was a bilingual congregation. The early service was in German, and the second in English. World War II ended the German service, and the leaders never could agree on a new identity. The second church was founded in 1908 as a neighborhood church, but the automobile and the growth of suburbia after the war undercut its future. The third also was founded as a neighborhood church on the near north side about the same time. By the late 1940s, however, that part of the city was being rezoned for commercial uses. After several years of conversations, leaders of the three churches began to talk about merging. That came to a head in mid-1953, when one of the three pastors was killed in an automobile accident. A month later the third announced he would be retiring at the end of August. A few months earlier the pastor of what had been that German church announced he and his wife were getting a divorce, and he would be leaving the professional ministry."

"When did you come on the scene?" I inquired.

"We arrived on September 1, 1953. I was 29 years old and in my fourth year as the associate minister of a big downtown church in Jackson," recalled this pastor. "I had no intention of leaving there, but a delegation of nine leaders from these three churches came to see me. They explained they had abandoned the idea of merger. Instead, they wanted to unite to create a new congregation with a new name at a new location and carve out a new future."

"What's the difference between a merger and a union?" I asked.

"That was one of my first questions," explained this pastor, who clearly was eager to share that distinction. "They explained that after about four years of conversations about merger, the negotiations had broken down because they could not agree on which buildings to sell, on a name for the new merged church, on who would be the permanent pastor, on how to terminate the employment of the other two ministers, and a dozen other divisive issues. A few days before what looked like it would be their last joint meeting, it turned out there would be three pulpit vacancies. At that meeting one of the wisest people I've ever met suggested their problem was a consequence of focusing on means-to-an-end issues such as real estate, staffing, local traditions, money, and other accumulated assets. He urged the group to abandon the goal of merging these three congregations because that naturally tended to create conflict over the allocation of resources, including leadership roles."

"That fits a common pattern," I interrupted. "Most discussions in the churches on means-to-an-end issues such as governance, real estate, money, staffing, and schedules tend to be divisive. What did this person suggest?"

"He urged them to replace that old topic of merger and focus on church union. That is an old term that has been around for generations, but usually is applied to denominational mergers, not to congregations," replied this pastor. "While it took an hour or two for everyone to get on board, by the time that meeting adjourned they had agreed to abandon efforts toward merger, replace that with the new goal of union, and look for a pastor to lead them down this new road. That's when they came to see me."

"Why did they pick you?" my curiosity prompted me to inquire.

"That's what I asked," recalled this pastor. "As I told you a couple of minutes ago, I was happy where I was and had no intention of moving. They gave me five reasons. First, their vision called for this new congregation to become a big church. By the time they came to see me, all three congregations had agreed union, not merger, was the road to their future. They had an option to purchase a 7-acre site at an excellent site, and also had purchase offers for two of their churches. Therefore they wanted their new minister to be someone with experience in a large church. The combined worship attendance of their three congregations at that time was about 160. They wanted a minister who was comfortable with a congregation two or three times that size. Second, they recognized this would be a long-term process, so they wanted a young minister. Third, they saw families with young children as their number-one future constituency. At the time we had two children, ages 4 and 2, so we matched that requirement. Fourth, they really examined me at great length to be sure that I understood their distinction between merger and union, that I was in full agreement with their vision of what tomorrow could bring, and that I believed God was truly calling me to come and help them fulfill their vision. A week later when I came here for a second interview, a couple of members really pushed hard on this issue of call. Finally, they explained they did not want a minister who was eager to leave his present assignment. They wanted a pastor who was happy where he was, not one who was looking to be bailed out."

"Bring me up to date," I urged. "Tell me what happened."

"Next month will mark our 16th anniversary here for my wife and me.

"We sold all three properties during my first couple of months and spent two years meeting in the local high school. That turned out to be a real blessing. Too often merged churches agree to use the best building and sell the other one or two. That immediately creates winners and losers. The losers are those who gave up their sacred meeting place. The winners are the ones who not only were able to continue to worship in their familiar place, but also that building reinforced the power of the culture of that congregation. Selling all three parcels of land eliminated that problem. The high school became neutral turf not only for our people, but also for first-time visitors. In addition, that dependence on a temporary meeting place reinforced the future orientation in the culture of this united congregation. Creating a new church together unified our people. There also is no question but that I undergirded that future orientation. For all practical purposes, I carried zero memories of the past.

"Sixteen years and three building programs later, our combined attendance at three weekend worship services averages 615, about the same as it was in my former church in Jackson when I left there in 1953," continued this pastor.

"I don't know about you, but I would call that a success story," I observed.

"I wouldn't!" declared the pastor in a very determined tone of voice. "First, I do not believe attendance should be the primary criterion in defining success. Second, we won't know how this story really turns out until at least six or seven years after the arrival of my successor. I am convinced that my gifts, skills, personality, theological stance, priorities in ministry, age, marital status, and leadership style turned out to be close to a perfect match for what these three congregations needed at that point in their history. Let's not call it a success until a few years after the arrival of the next senior minister."

That interview took place in 1969.

That also was this traveler's first introduction to the difference between merger and union.[1]

Inputs or Outcomes?

Thirty-plus years later additional experiences have under-scored the differences. Congregational mergers tend to be based on a widely shared assumption there is a shortage of resources. They tend to be driven by a desire to perpetuate the past rather than create the new. They tend to cause the leaders to focus on means-to-an-end issues and on inputs rather than on desired future outcomes. Mergers tend to force compromise on values, traditions, and goals. They tend to assume the new merged con-gregation should be defined in terms of geography rather than demographics or unmet needs or ideology or theology or a defi-nition of mission.

All too often two small Protestant congregations are urged to merge on the assumption that combining weakness and a pes-simistic view of the future with weakness and another pessimistic view of tomorrow will produce strength, hope, and a bright future. Chapters 6, 7, 8, 10, and 12 suggest that a more produc-tive strategy builds on strength and hope.

The merger of two congregations each averaging 60 to 70 at worship tends to perpetuate a small-church culture rather than replace that old culture with a midsized church culture. One fre-quent consequence is 65 plus 70 usually ends up producing a merged congregation that a few years later averages fewer than 100 at worship. Similarly the merger of the very small church averaging 35 at worship with one averaging 100 or more usually means the larger church swallows up the smaller one, gulps twice, and plateaus with the same culture and at the same size it was before. Likewise, if the merger brings together one congregation with a comfortable size and well-maintained meeting place, and another with a badly deteriorated building or one that has been destroyed by a fire or flood or tornado, the natural pattern is for the comfortable congregation to swallow up those permanent visitors, gulp only once, and continue on as it was before.

The most successful congregational unions tend to be those involving three congregations, no one of which represents a majority of the constituents, and everyone agrees the goal is to create a new congregation under a new name with a new role and identity that will meet in a new (at least new to all participating congregations) meeting place with a new definition of the primary constituency, a powerful future-driven policy-making process (rather than to perpetuate or re-create the past), and new ministerial leadership. Ideally that new minister will bring an entrepreneurial leadership style plus firsthand experiences with a congregation similar in size, type, and role to what this union is expected to produce. The ideal tenure for that new minister will be closer to three decades than to only one decade.

On the other hand, congregational mergers can be one component of a larger denominational strategy that (1) assumes the easiest and most effective way to reach new constituencies is with new missions; (2) believes mergers are preferable to dissolutions in reducing the number of what have been identified as redundant or obsolete congregations; (3) is experiencing a shortage of pastors or ministerial teams who bring the gifts, skills, leadership ability, vision, persuasive communication, patience, experience, optimism, and determination required to transform the congregation founded in 1963 or earlier that now averages fewer than a hundred at worship into a church that can attract substantial numbers of newcomers in today's highly competitive, ecclesiastical marketplace; (4) expects to plant at least one new mission for every congregation that disappears through dissolution or merger; (5) relies on a national rather than a regional inventory of pastors in the search for clergy able and willing to lead those merger processes; or (6) has decided to reduce its presence in that region, state, county, city, or community.

Congregational mergers also can be a useful component of the strategy for denominational mergers, if one long-term goal is to cut back on the number of churches. One example is what today is The United Methodist Church. In 1960 the two predecessor denominations included 43,400 congregations. (That was down from over 57,000 in 1906.) During the next four decades approximately 1,600 new missions were planted. Thanks to mergers, dissolutions, and a tiny number of withdrawals, by the end of 2000 the number of congregations in the new merged church had been reduced to 35,721—a reduction of 18 percent. Parallel patterns on a more modest scale followed the mergers that created the Evangelical Lutheran Church in America, the Presbyterian Church (U.S.A.), and the United Church of Christ.

Should your congregation consider a merger with another church? A better agenda is to agree on the desired outcome. Is it to attempt to perpetuate the past? Or, to join with other future-oriented Christians who are motivated by a compelling vision of creating a new tomorrow?

CHAPTER FOURTEEN

THREE TECHNOLOGICAL SCENARIOS

In 1920, approximately 8 million privately owned motor vehicles were in use in the United States. Eighty years later that number had increased to 135 million. One consequence has been an increase in the length of the journey to work for tens of millions of Americans from a few hundred yards or less to many miles. Another consequence has been the undermining of traditional neighborhood institutions such as the corner drugstore, the family owned and -operated grocery store, the one-screen neighborhood motion picture theater, the physician with his office in his home, the neighborhood post office, the five-and-dime variety store on Main Street, the lodge hall, the small locally owned neighborhood bank, the public elementary school with 50 to 200 pupils, and the church. Most have been replaced by much larger and more impersonal regional institutions.

Earlier the combination of the telegraph, the railroads, the Civil War, internal migration, the telephone, the mail order catalog, and radio had transformed a collection of states, territories, and scattered settlements into one nation. That created the cultural and political context for the emergence of nationwide Protestant denominations, which flourished for a hundred years following the Civil War. Many of the earlier regional denomina-

163

tional judicatories that had been defined on the basis of ancestry were replaced by regional judicatories defined by state or county boundaries.

Which of these many technological changes had the greatest impact on American Protestant congregations during the 20th century? Was it the widespread ownership of the private motor vehicle? Or, was it the easy availability and relatively low price of electricity? Or, was it television that raised the bar on people's expectations of worship and preaching? Or, was it radio that popularized one approach to public speaking in the 1925–1985 era that has since been replaced by television's model of effective oral communication?[1] (By 1990 television had made obsolete the old practice of reading sermons from manuscripts. Television has taught new generations of viewers that oral communication comes accompanied by projected visual images and/or wrapped in entertainment.)

Or, more recently, did the greatest impact arrive when email made letter writing a lost art and greatly reduced the delay in receiving a response to an inquiry? Or, was it the combination of shopping malls, cable television, affluence, personal computers, the Internet, and consumerism that taught younger generations a plethora of choices is a natural right, along with life, liberty, education, excellent health care, and a comfortable retirement?

From this traveler's perspective, three recent technological changes will have a tremendous impact on the future of American Protestantism. One is television and videotapes. Television enables viewers "to be there without being there," often in real time. The crash of those two commercial aircraft into the twin towers on September 11, 2001, remains a living memory for billions who have never been to New York City. Videotapes now give every interested congregation easy access to the highest quality preaching available anywhere. Likewise, technological advances in the recording industry have made inspirational Christian music, both vocal and instrumental, readily accessible. That is another valuable technological resource.

The second technological miracle is that distance education is replacing the traditional residential institution of higher education. This opens the door to those free agents identified in chapter 6 to acquire the formal education required for their new careers. The unresolved question is not "When?" but "Who?" Who will provide this to that growing constituency?

The third technological miracle is the Internet. For most of American church history, parishioners not only saw one another in church, they also encountered fellow church members during the week at work, at the post office, on the street, at funerals and weddings, at the general store, and in visits with kinfolk. The consequence was, the grapevine worked. It was an effective channel of communication. Urbanization has been accompanied by a geographical scattering of the membership. The replacement of small neighborhood institutions by large regional ones, plus the geographical separation of the place of residence from the place of work, undermined the speed and reliability of the grapevine. To compensate for the deterioration of the grapevine, large regional churches have budgeted the printing and distribution by mail of a weekly parish newsletter, but that is too costly for most congregations. The personal computer, the Internet, and the congregation's own website (or the use of a member's email address) have now made it possible for nearly every congregation to benefit from a reliable, low-cost, fast, and accessible channel of communication to replace that old grapevine. The website also opens the door for every member to be a reporter or contributing editor. This can be replaced or supplemented by a 10-minute videotape shown just before the beginning of the worship service that recaptures what happened during the past week in the lives of the people in the worshiping community and announces coming events.

What's Next?

What will the future bring to those 3,000 American Protestant congregations that report their worship attendance averages 12? Or, the thousand that average 11? Together they are as numerous as those averaging a thousand or more at worship. What does the future hold for those 4,000 American Protestant congregations averaging 20 at worship? Or, the 13,000 others averaging between 21 and 25 at worship?

The best answer is, "It all depends." For those that are perceived by their denominational policy makers to be redundant or obsolete or irrelevant, merger, sharing a pastor with one or more other churches, or dissolution may be what the future holds for them. The future also may be bleak for those in which the congregational culture is dominated by nostalgia, despair, passivity, hopelessness, and pessimism. Likewise, those small congregations in which the leaders are convinced their ministry requires the services of a full-time, seminary-trained resident pastor may enter a future filled with frustration and disappointment.

On the other hand, the future has never been brighter for those small churches in which the members (1) describe paved roads and automobiles as assets; (2) have accumulated thousands of hours of practice watching projected visual images on motion picture, television, and/or computer screens; (3) include at least one person, perhaps a high school student or a retiree, who is skilled in the use of modern media; (4) place a high value on intimacy and the absence of complexity; (5) demand high-quality preaching and inspirational music; (6) choose a church home on the basis of variables other than geographical convenience, or one that has "a great Sunday school where we can drop off the kids while we go shopping on Sunday morning"; (7) do not believe "it can't be church if we don't have our own full-time ordained minister"; (8) are comfortable with the ministry of the laity; (9) are not threatened by the fact that many people, including some of their friends, neighbors, and relatives, prefer a large "full-service church"; and most important of all, (10) display an attitude of optimism, hope, and openness to "new ways of doing church" as they look to the future.

Three Scenarios

Perhaps the smoothest road into the future already has been opened to those very small Protestant congregations in which the members (1) place a high value on retaining complete autonomy over their planning; (2) do not need or seek any financial subsidies; (3) include three to seven lay volunteers who are willing and able to be trained as worship leaders, lay ministers, and leaders of adult classes; (4) display a low level of dependency and a relatively high level of entrepreneurial gifts ("We can do that ourselves."); (5) are open to utilizing modern technology; and (6) place a high value on excellent preaching. The combination of those assets and expectations can enable those very small congregations to carve out a promising future. The only other major variable in this option is their meeting place. Do they own a conventional church building? If yes, can they afford to operate it and maintain it? Or, is it a "white elephant" inherited from the past? Or, should they rent space from another congregation? Or meet in a storefront? Or in a large room at the nearby college, bank, school, lodge hall, or in the office building where several members are employed? Or in a private home?

Those larger congregations averaging 25 to 60 or more at worship may want to sacrifice total autonomy in order to acquire full access to other ministries and services. A second scenario depicts how that can be achieved by choosing to affiliate with a full-service church described earlier in chapter 7. This scenario does require taking the initiative in searching for a partner.

Regardless of size, those small churches in which there is a shortage of entrepreneurial and self-confident lay volunteers ready and able to accept new responsibilities may prefer a third scenario. This requires asking a self-identified missionary church (see chapter 6) to adopt them. This can give them access to a variety of resources, ministries, programs, and activities without surrendering their traditional role as a gathered community of Christians coming together to worship God, to care for one another, and to serve as a surrogate family for many. One variation in this third scenario calls for that small congregation to retain complete control over and responsibility for the operation and maintenance of their real estate. A more radical change requires title to the real estate to be transferred to that missionary church.

Two Questions

In terms of supply and demand, will the number of small churches seeking to affiliate with a large full-service congregation or to build a relationship with a self-identified missionary church exceed the number of larger churches able and willing to fulfill that role? Or, will those larger churches prepare themselves to meet a demand that does not materialize?

One perspective declares that will be determined by denominational initiatives. Will denominational policy makers challenge larger churches to choose one of these two roles? Will policy makers encourage small congregations to consider this type of relationship?

This observer's experiences suggest the nondenominational churches at both ends of the size spectrum are more likely to pursue these scenarios than are denominationally affiliated congregations. One explanation is, all three scenarios can be perceived as threats to denominational loyalty. If a congregation seeks and receives the help it needs from a large church, will one consequence be an increase in institutional loyalty to that partner congregation, with a resulting decrease in loyalty to denominational headquarters?

That concern is based on reality! While no one can prove a cause-and-effect relationship, it may not be a coincidence that as an increasing number of mainline Protestant congregations have turned to parachurch organizations, retreat centers, self-identified teaching churches, independent publishing houses, profit-driven corporations, nondenominational missionary-sending agencies, and nondenominational theological schools for

resources; their loyalty to their own denomination has deteriorated. Can these denominations enhance intradenominational
loyalty by a greater emphasis on providing innovative and relevant resources to congregations? Or, does that concept fit into
the same category as the small dairy farm, the one-car garage, the
small public high school, and the family-owned and -operated
general store?

That introduces the second unknown. Who will provide the
videotapes of those meaningful and memorable sermons? Who
will provide the recorded music? Who will equip those lay free
agents to accept and fulfill new responsibilities? Will these
resources be created and made available largely on an intradenominational basis? Or, will the new American ecclesiastical free
market produce a variety of vendors across denominational lines?
Will that self-identified teaching church make its resources available only to congregations affiliated with its denominational tradition? Or, will those teaching churches and missionary
congregations compete across denominational boundaries with
theological schools, parachurch organizations, individual entre-
preneurs, retreat centers, nondenominational publishing houses,
and others in creating and distributing these resources?

CHAPTER FIFTEEN

A DOZEN REALLY HARD CASES

The largest 30 percent of congregations in American Protestantism account for 70 percent of the people who worship with a Protestant church on the typical weekend. The remaining 70 percent account for only 30 percent of those worshipers. What is the future for that 70 percent? What is the future for those congregations that average somewhere between 2 and 125 at worship?

The central thesis of this book is that the vast majority of the 225,000 small Protestant congregations in America have the freedom, within some limits of course, to shape their own future. The resources, options, and opportunities for a Christian church in America have never been as plentiful, as useful, as challenging, and as varied as they are today. One basis for that optimistic statement is the 50-year-old American-born reader who can say, "The number of self-identified Christians in America has nearly doubled during my lifetime."

On the other hand, the competition among the churches to reach and attract future constituents also is at an all-time high. (See chapter 4.) A visit to the real world suggests that one consequence of this competition is the majority of the small Protestant congregations in existence in America on December 31, 1990, followed one of five paths during the 1990s. One group had dissolved sometime during the decade of the 1990s. A second group merged with, and often into, another congregation. The majority experienced a significant decrease in their average worship attendance. A fourth and the second largest group remained, more or less, on a plateau in size; the fifth group reported an increase of more than 10 percent in their average worship attendance.

While differences in these studies in the time span covered and in the denominational tradition analyzed make it impossible to come up with one precise generalization, the evidence suggests that two-thirds of the congregations averaging fewer than 50 at worship in 1990 chose one of the first three of those options, as did one-half of those averaging 50 to 125 at worship in 1990.

That does not mean those will be heavily traveled roads for small churches during the first and second decades of the 21st century. The vast majority of the 225,000 congregations in this small-church category can, if the members so desire, choose a more attractive road into the future. The resources are available, and the opportunities are many. A small minority, however, represent what can be described as hard cases. A dozen examples will illustrate the variety of these cases.

1. A Shrinking Population

Approximately one-fifth of the 3,000-plus counties experienced a decrease in population during the 1990s. A common ratio is 1 Christian congregation for every 300 residents, most of whom are both willing and able to travel 8 to 12 miles each way to church. The competition means the surviving congregations in 2020 will be drawn largely from among (a) the larger congregations that can offer a combination of relevance, quality, and choices, and (b) the smaller churches that carve out a precisely defined niche and excel in that niche.

One example is Faith Church. It was founded in 1920 to serve the residents of a newly emerging neighborhood. Most of the adult males in that neighborhood were employed by a nearby factory that opened in 1924. By 1929 this new mission was meeting in its new brick building and averaging 95 at worship. That factory survived the Great Depression but cut its labor force by half. Defense orders in the 1940s brought additions to the factory, and by 1945 the number of employees was double the 1928 level. In 1953, worship attendance at Faith Church peaked at 210, and a three-story Sunday school addition was built to replace the old parsonage. Employment at the factory dropped during the 1960s and 1970s, but it continued to be the number-one employer in the local economy. New generations of workers came from all over the city rather than from that neighborhood.

The members at Faith Church have been growing older and fewer in numbers. Their last full-time pastor retired in mid-1988. The average worship attendance in 1989 was 68. Faith Church was served by a seminary student followed by a retired minister followed by a college professor who served as the weekend minister followed by another seminary student in the 1988–2001 period. In early 2001 the factory closed. The work was being transferred to a factory in Alabama.

Worship attendance at Faith Church had been slowly declining and averaged 47 in 2000. Twenty households provided nearly all the dollars for that $56,000 budget in 2000. During 2001 and 2002, seven of the 15 largest contributors disappeared. Two died, three couples chose early retirement and moved out of town. The largest contributor accepted an attractive offer to move with the factory to Alabama as a division chief. The third largest contributor took a better job, but had to move to another city. By late 2002 church attendance was down to 34, and the proposed budget for 2003 was $33,000.

Four of the other five churches in that county that were affiliated with Faith Church's denomination have experienced at least a 15 percent decrease in church attendance since 1998. What course of action should the leaders at Faith Church choose?

2. Hopelessness

Overlapping that first category are the small churches that can be found in every urban, suburban, or rural county. In these congregations a compelling vision of a new tomorrow is buried under a huge mound of despair and hopelessness.

As was pointed out in the introduction, the absence of hope may be the motivation to choose the road that leads to dissolution. In the average week at least 30 Protestant congregations choose that option, some of them located in communities experiencing continued population growth.

3. The Obsolescence of Purpose

"This parish goes back to 1890, when it was founded by a Lutheran pastor from Denmark to serve the Danish Lutherans migrating to this county." That pastor is dead. Those passenger ships from Denmark have been sold for scrap. The grandchildren and great-grandchildren of those Danish immigrants do not use a hyphen in describing their own identity. They are Americans! During the past 60 years, nine consecutive pastors have been unable to persuade that passing parade of members to redefine their identity and role. One third-generation member explained, "Next month I'll be 80 years old, and I expect to be buried in the cemetery next to this church. Our responsibility as a parish is to maintain this cemetery." That is not a high priority among the current unchurched residents of that community.

4. Denial

"We don't have a problem. The problem is with younger generations who are too busy to find a place for the church in their lives. As they grow older, they'll discover the importance of religion, and we'll be here waiting to welcome and serve them."

5. The Rich Uncle

"My uncle Jim is the grandson of the couple who founded this church. Over the years he has accumulated a lot of money. Last year he contributed over half of the money we needed to cover our expenses. This congregation doesn't have to worry about its future as long as Uncle Jim is around to pick up the tab."

6. Short Pastorates

"Our current minister is the seventh in nine years. Of the six predecessors, the first resigned to move to Arizona to be near his wife's aging parents. The second was defrocked when it was discovered he was embezzling money from the Pastor's Emergency Aid account. The third left in the middle of what turned out to be a messy divorce. The fourth left after only a year to become the associate minister in the church in which he had been reared. The fifth was killed in an automobile accident. The sixth was caught downloading pornography on the office computer and told to resign; and our seventh arrived three months ago. Our specialty is giving parties to welcome new pastors. That's what we do best, but I'm afraid others have concluded there is something wrong with this congregation."

7. "We're in Mission"

"It's true that our average worship attendance has dropped from about 110 in 1990 to 58 last year, but that's a poor yardstick to use in evaluating a church. The only valid yardstick is mission. We focus on mission in this community. We house a weekday childcare program in our building five days a week. The woman who organized and runs it pays all our utility and insurance bills and gives the church an additional $500 a month that we use toward the salary of our part-time minister. We are one of eight churches in a coalition formed here about 10 years ago to provide a food pantry and a clothes closet for the needy. One of our two first-floor classrooms has an outside entrance that houses the food pantry, which is stocked by these eight churches. That other first-floor classroom is now used to store donated used clothing. Both are open for three hours every Saturday morning and are staffed by volunteers from these cooperating congregations. On the third Thursday of every month, except July and August, our big first-floor fellowship hall is used from 6:00 in the evening until 8:00 in the morning to shelter the homeless. Another church provides the volunteer staff for that ministry, while we provide the space and utilities. We also house the weekly or monthly meetings of a dozen community organizations that meet here evenings. That long list includes Alcoholics Anonymous, a Divorce Recovery Group, a mutual support group for substance abusers, Amnesty International, a weight-loss group, and several others. We also host a dinner for a Tuesday evening service club, and our women clear about $3,500 a year from that. In addition, a whole variety of other community organizations use our building on Saturdays, and a small Korean congregation rents it from noon to 5:00 every Sunday. You'll have to look a long way before you'll find a busier building than ours! Our focus is on mission to this community, not on evangelism. We have taken literally the biblical mandate to feed the hungry, clothe the naked, shelter the homeless, and provide a safe haven for children. That may not be the road to church growth, but we believe we're called to be in mission to the people in this community, even if that doesn't produce numerical growth."

A long chapter in the history of the Christian church suggests a high degree of compatibility between clothing the naked, feeding the hungry, sheltering the homeless, and caring for children with the proclamation of the gospel of Jesus Christ. It is easy, however, for that landlord role to take over the agenda.

8. The Price Tag on Intrachurch Quarrels

In recent decades several of the larger American Protestant denominations have demonstrated that highly visible and divisive intradenominational quarrels tend to be incompatible with numerical growth. While they may watch from a substantial institutional distance, the vast majority of American adults tend to avoid becoming involved in any organization that has chosen up sides in order to turn a difference of opinion into a highly divisive public quarrel. That generalization applies to political parties, profit-driven corporations, professional sports teams, religious bodies, hospitals, service clubs, and other voluntary associations, including religious congregations.

Internal quarreling has not turned out to be an effective strategy for attracting new constituents. How does a congregation that excels in highly visible internal quarrels attract new members? That question may have an answer, but it will not be found in this book!

9. The Impact of Long-term Financial Subsidies

Long ago, economists came up with this advice: "That which is taxed tends to disappear, while that which is subsidized tends to increase."

The Episcopal Church in the United States has had a long history of demonstrating that this generalization also applies to congregations. The United Methodist Church also has provided evidence for the validity of this rule. More recently this advice has been used to explain the disappearance of the small family farm and the growth of the heavily subsidized corporate farms, which have used federal subsidies to price the small family farmer out of the marketplace. Long-term financial subsidies appear to be incompatible with the numerical growth of small Protestant churches.

10. Parking Can Be a Problem

Second Church was founded in 1907 by the members at First Church to serve the residents of a newly developing neighborhood on the near east side of the city. In 1945 the new pastor at Second Church saw a brighter future by relocating to a better site. In 1951 Second Church moved into a highly functional two-story building on a 60,000-square-foot parcel of land 3 miles north of the old site. This new site was in the middle of a new neighborhood of new single family homes which, in 1951, were selling for $16,000 to $18,000. This new site was directly across the street from a new public elementary school that opened for classes in the fall of 1950. By 1960 Second Church was averaging nearly 300 at worship and was clearly the favorite congregation of residents of that neighborhood. The Sunday school addition constructed in 1962 was easily paid for, but that did reduce the number of church-owned parking spaces from 53 to 22.

The minister who had led the relocation process retired in 1983. He was followed by an unintentional interim minister who served for two years, a mature minister who retired in 1993, a recent seminary graduate who left in 1998, and the current pastor who arrived in mid-1998.

In 1987 a court order mandated an open-enrollment policy for that public school district. That meant any student could enroll in the appropriate grade school in any school in the district. One consequence was three-quarters of the student body at this elementary school now arrive by bus from outside this neighborhood.

The houses constructed in 1949 to 1952 are now more than 50 years old. The one-car family has been replaced by households with two or three vehicles. Street parking is scarce, especially on Sunday mornings. Those 53 offstreet parking spaces owned by the church in the 1950s, plus the available nearby street parking, were adequate in 1960 when worship attendance averaged 300. When church attendance exceeds 115, which now happens

178

about 30 Sundays a year, every one of those remaining 22 spaces is filled.

Nearly everyone agrees that the current pastor, who arrived in 1998, is an exceptionally gifted preacher, a loving shepherd, and a great teacher who displays an attractive personality.

Homes adjacent to Second Church's property do come on the market, but the deed restrictions limit the use of those lots to single family homes. That means Second Church cannot add the offstreet parking required to redefine its role into a regional congregation.

11. The Resistance to Change

"During my five years as the pastor here, we have created three long range planning committees," explained a pastor in his letter of resignation. "The first one concluded we do not have a viable future here on this site and recommended we relocate. When that recommendation was presented to a congregational meeting, the result was 89 votes in favor of relocation and 93 votes against. Eighteen months later a new long-range planning committee studied our situation and also concluded we could not perpetuate the past into the future without more parking. They recommended we purchase four adjacent properties, raze the buildings, and pave the land for offstreet parking. When that was presented to the congregation, the vote was 73 in favor and 88 against. Two months ago a third special planning committee also agreed that the present situation is not viable, and they recommended we lease two vacant stores in a strip shopping center 2 miles east of here and become a two-site church. The congregational vote was 62 in favor and 69 against. I have concluded that the admonition 'Three strikes and you're out!' also applies to parish pastors, so I am resigning my ministry here effective on the last day of next month."

One response to that series of experiences is, do not waste your time with people who refuse to change. A better diagnosis is, "Rejection is the natural, normal, and predictable response to a new idea the first time it is presented. When should we bring this up again, and what must we do to prepare people to make a wise and future-oriented decision?"

The best strategy, when it is clear the status quo no longer is a viable road to the future, is not to offer that as an option. Do not ask people to choose between yes and no. That conveys the impression that the status quo is a viable option. Ask them to choose between Change A and Change B. For example, the question could be, "Do you favor opening the door to reaching new generations by relocating our meeting place, or do you favor continued numerical decline and eventual dissolution by continuing here as our meeting place?"

Four Critical Questions

12. Apathy

What can be done when the congregation is marked by apathy and no one displays any hope for the future? Maybe dissolve?

From a denominational perspective, one source of these hard cases can be traced back to four questions.

First, what do you believe will be the most effective way to proclaim the gospel of Jesus Christ and evangelize new generations in the 21st century? Will small churches be the most effective strategy? Or large and very large congregations? (See point 4 of chapter 4.)

Your answer to that question introduces the second question. This question is based on a key assumption in systems theory. Every system produces the outcomes it is designed to produce. These may not be the outcomes desired by those who operate the system, but these are the outcomes the system is designed to produce. In New York City, for example, the system in place in 2001 and 2002 was designed to produce competition and conflict between the uniformed police officers and the city's firefighters.

That was not a desired outcome, but that is what the system was designed to produce.

The third question can be summarized in 15 words: Is your denominational system designed to produce more very large churches or more small congregations?

The Southern Baptist Convention, the Seventh-day Adventist Church, the Episcopal Church USA, and The United Methodist Church represent four different religious bodies under that broad umbrella called American Protestantism. One point of commonality is all four are Trinitarian bodies. A second, but unrelated point of commonality is all four operate with an ecclesiastical system designed to produce a disproportionately large number of small congregations. These four systems vary in several respects, but all four are designed to produce similar outcomes.

This can be illustrated by looking at the United Methodist system. At the end of 1972, after four years on the shakedown cruise following the merger of 1968, this new denomination reported a total of 39,626 organized churches, down from 40,653 in 1970, and from approximately 44,000 in the two predecessor denominations in 1960. One facet of the system created by the merger of these two denominations was a bias in favor of the merger or dissolution of congregations.

For the calendar year 1972 a total of 3,830 United Methodist congregations reported an average worship attendance of fewer than 20; 5,792 reported an average worship attendance of 20 to 34; 28,010 reported an average worship attendance of 35 or more; and 1,984 did not report their worship attendance. Twenty-seven years later, at the end of 1999, the number of congregations had decreased by nearly 4,000 to 35,609, reflecting thousands of mergers and dissolutions. At least 1,200 new missions were launched during that 1973–1999 period, so the actual number of congregations that disappeared was well over 5,000. The system was producing what it was designed to produce—a reduction in the number of congregations.

For the calendar year 1999 a total of 4,630 congregations reported their average worship attendance was less than 20, an increase of 800 in the number of very small churches despite all those mergers and closings. The number reporting an average worship attendance of 20 to 34 had increased by 168 to 5,960. The number reporting an average worship attendance of 35 or more plunged from 28,010 in 1972 to 24,278 in 1999, while the number not reporting dropped to 741.

That United Methodist system was especially effective in reducing the number of congregations averaging 100 to 199 at worship. This is a bracket that often provides the first full-time appointment for seminary graduates. While the proportion of congregations reporting their average worship attendance rose, the number in this size bracket dropped from 7,468 in 1972 to 5,874 in 1999. The number of midsized churches reporting an average worship attendance of 200 to 349 dropped by over 400 from 2,943 in 1972 to 2,528 in 1999. The good news for United Methodists was the number averaging 350 or more at worship climbed from a total of 1,278, or 3.4 percent of all reporting congregations in 1972, to 1,585 in 1999, or 4.5 percent of all reporting their worship attendance.

That statistical review of one large mainline American Protestant denomination introduces the fourth of these four questions for denominational policy makers. If the current design of your denominational system is not producing the outcomes you desire, are you prepared to change the design? Thus if the policy makers in these four denominations mentioned earlier are convinced the future lies with the small church, they should be happy with their system that has produced and is producing a disproportionately large number of small churches.

To return to The United Methodist Church as an example, it is easy to identify several reasons why that system is biased toward (1) reducing the number of congregations and (2) increasing the proportion that average fewer than 35 at worship. A condensed list includes (1) an excessive number of mismatches between minister and congregations; (2) too many short pastorates of one to seven years (partly a consequence of so many mismatches) and too few pastorates of 10 to 40 (short pastorates tend to be incompatible with numerical growth, as the Seventh-day Adventists and others have discovered); (3) a reluctance to recognize the neighborhood church became obsolete back in the 1960s; (4) the dream that theological pluralism would be an inclusive force when it has turned out to be a divisive force; (5) the widespread use of a small-church model in designing new missions; (6) a growing distrust of local leadership, with the resulting conclusion the denomination should expand its role as a regulatory body; (7) a failure to challenge small congregations to choose from one of a score or more of different scenarios in designing its future, and an excessive reliance on dissolution, merger, a cooperative ministry, and circuits in which one minister serves two or more congregations concurrently as the four primary options; (8) providing a variety of public platforms for highly visible intradenominational quarrels; (9) giving a higher priority to the concerns of the clergy than to new church development (a modest goal would be to launch 200 new missions annually, with each designed to average 500 or more at worship by the end of the fifth year); (10) a reluctance to utilize modern technology such as projected visual imagery; (11) the operational assumption that regional judicatories should be defined by geography rather than by affinity; (12) a reluctance to encourage the emergence of more self-identified teaching churches to enable congregational leaders to learn from one another; (13) the dream that denominationally allocated financial subsidies will be an asset rather than a deterrent to change; (14) a reluctance to encourage large churches to become multisite congregations; (15) an excessively short tenure for district superintendents that is a barrier to their being able to help congregations design and implement a customized ministry plan; (16) a reluctance by annual conferences to prepare and circulate among congregational leaders an annual performance audit of the ministry of that conference (thus not opening the door for informed and constructive criticism from highly competent congregational leaders); (17) a reluctance to challenge congregations that have been meeting for several decades in what is now a functionally obsolete building on an inadequate site at what is now a poor location to relocate to a new meeting place as part of a larger strategy to begin a new volume in that congregation's history; (18) expecting congregations to resource denominational goals rather than designing the denominational systems to resource congregations; (19) using the apportionment system to "tax" numerical growth and/or good stewardship, and using financial benefits to reward numerical decline and/or incompetence; (20) assuming that, by virtue of election, bishops automatically will be endowed with the gifts and skills required for responsibilities in the allocation of human resources; and, perhaps most serious of all, (21) the operational assumption that more continuing education for pastors will cure the problem. This not only places an unrealistic expectation on classroom education, it also tends to identify the ministers as the source of "our problems" rather than to begin to reform what has become a dysfunctional system.

In summary, if you believe your denomination includes an excessive number of small congregations, reform the system so it will stop giving birth to more. One common theme that surfaces in most of these hard cases is the temptation to perpetuate yesterday. The $10 term for this syndrome is path dependency. Once a path has been defined, institutions naturally tend to be attracted to that same path. That generalization applies to American foreign policy, what people choose to eat for lunch, how parents attempt to rear that second child, and how we try to do church in the context of a changing culture.

CHAPTER SIXTEEN

A
DENOMINATIONAL
PERSPECTIVE

Most of the larger American Protestant denominations report that, give or take 12 percentage points, 60 percent of their affiliated congregations average fewer than 100 at worship. How should the national and regional agencies of the denomination relate to these congregations? The best answer is, "That depends."

A better beginning point is to agree on the top priority for that denomination in the early years of this new millennium. For this discussion, let us begin with four assumptions. First, there is value in a denomination rallying behind one top priority and creating the decision-making processes to make this possible. The agenda will include other goals and priorities, but the same one is at the top of both the national and regional lists of goals and priorities. (At this point we may have lost several readers who have died of laughter.)

Second, widespread agreement on a single top priority makes it easier to allocate scarce resources such as paid personnel, money, energy, time, and volunteers.

Third, the pressures of intradenominational politics will prohibit the future of "our small churches" from becoming the top priority.

Fourth, the definition of that top priority will influence the relationship between congregations of all sizes and types, and the regional and national agencies of that denomination.

Nine Scenarios

This beginning point can be illustrated by looking briefly at nine different top denominational priorities and speculating on the response of most small congregations.

1. The top denominational priority is to produce a net annual increase of at least 10 percent in membership in this denomination. The two key components of an effective strategy probably will be (a) to plant at least two new missions every year for every 100 existing congregations in this denomination, and (b) every five years double the number of affiliated congregations averaging at least 800 at worship. The explanation is younger generations of Protestant churchgoers can be found in disproportionately large numbers in new missions and/or very large churches.

The leaders in the vast majority of small churches will shrug, "That's fine with us as long as you don't invade our territory or ask us for money."

2. The top denominational priority is to produce a net annual increase in membership by every congregation, regardless of size, to increase its membership by 10 percent annually.

The leaders in most small churches probably will respond, "That's a great idea for our large churches, but obviously you don't expect us to grow at that rate. We'll be happy to continue on a plateau in size. We don't have the resources required to meet that goal."

The denominational leaders explain, "Yes, we do mean you! And we're prepared to help you design and implement a customized ministry plan that will produce that outcome. All we need from you is an invitation to come and help you."

At least half of the small churches do not extend that invitation. (See chapter 11 for an explanation.)

3. The top denominational priority is to become a multicultural denomination. The leaders in the small churches reply, "Great! Do you plan to accomplish that by creating multicultural regional judicatories consisting of a variety of monocultural congregations? Or by creating multicultural regional judicatories with many new multicultural missions? Or by creating nongeographical regional judicatories, with each serving a specific ethnic minority constituency?[1] We're curious about which approach you plan to use, since only the third would affect us."

4. The top denominational priority is to promote ecumenism by opening the door to full pulpit and altar fellowship with other Christian traditions.

The leaders in the small churches probably will conclude, "We don't see how that would affect us, except maybe that it would increase our options when we seek a new minister." (The opposition probably will come from leaders in large congregations who see this as an unnecessary and unwelcome dilution of their religious identity.)

5. The decision is to move social justice issues to the top of the denominational agenda.

Most of the members in the majority of the small churches will ignore this decision. A few will applaud. Others will protest, "Who gave them the right to declare they are speaking for me?"

6. The top denominational priority is to make this a better world for children.

The members in most small churches will (a) applaud this decision, (b) be curious how the larger churches with discretionary resources will implement this priority, and (c) agree to a special financial appeal to raise $10 per member to be sent to denominational headquarters for helping children on other continents.

7. The denominational policy makers agree that (a) globalization is real, (b) the old colonial approach to world missions is obsolete, and (c) the top denominational priority will be to encourage every congregation to build a continuing relationship with at least two or three sister churches, or with new missions affiliated with our denomination on other continents. One facet

of this will be for every congregation to send teams of short-term missionaries (eight to 15 days) to be engaged in ministry with fellow Christians in these sister churches. Eventually Christians from these sister churches will visit their American partner congregation.[2]

Most of the members in the small churches will approve this, but regret that their congregation has neither the people nor the resources required for these ventures. A few will look to partner with a large church nearby and participate with that congregation. Others will lament, "We really should give top priority to helping churches like our own first, but I guess that's too much to expect."

8. An examination of the denominational budgets suggests the top priority focuses on ministerial leadership. This includes continuing education experiences for pastors, improved pensions and health care for retired ministers, health insurance for the clergy, a counseling center for troubled ministers and their families, financial subsidies for underpaid pastors, and grants to theological schools to equip the next generation of parish pastors and scholarships for students.

One response by members of small churches will be, "That's good! We need to take better care of our pastors." A second will be, "Can we get some of those subsidy dollars for our pastor?" A third will be, "That doesn't affect us, since we have a part-time lay pastor who has a full-time secular job."

9. The denominational policy makers are dismayed by the increase in congregational autonomy; by the way many of the very large churches are ignoring denominational mandates, policies, and traditions; and by the emergence of powerful unofficial caucuses and interest groups. The obvious response to this increase in intradenominational adversarial relationships is to restructure the entire denominational system. The vast majority of the members of the small congregations display zero interest in participating in these intradenominational quarrels, and only a few are involved in the restructuring process.

While none of these imaginary scenarios bear any resemblance to the real world of denominational policy making, all nine illustrate a single point from the perspective of most members of the small denominationally affiliated American Protestant congregations. They feel they have been the recipients of benign neglect. The big exception is when they believe the denomination has been too aggressive in encouraging mergers.

Two Other Scenarios

1. The denominational policy makers agree that one explanation for this very large number of small congregations can be traced to the impact of two factors. One is too often these small churches have a long history of pastorates of one to seven years. The other is the related consequence of an excessive number of mismatches between the gifts, skills, experience, personality, career goals, and priorities of the new minister, and the needs of that congregation if it is going to fulfill its potential.

A widespread, and excessively simplistic, explanation for what appears to be an increasing number of these mismatches often is described as "a shortage of competent and committed pastors who are in the ministry because they love the Lord rather than for the money."

A better diagnosis lifts up three factors. First, the level of competence required to be an effective parish pastor today is far higher than it was in the 1930s or 1950s or 1980s. The higher expectations churchgoers bring to church, the greater competition for people's time, energy, and money; the increased competition among Christian congregations in America to attract and retain new constituents, the impact of technology on communication, preaching, learning, and fellowship, and the replacement of the neighborhood congregation by the regional church have made the role of the parish pastor far more demanding than it was a generation or two ago. It also is unrealistic to expect residential seminaries that identify themselves as graduate schools of theology, rather than as professional schools, to be able to prepare students to be effective parish pastors in the 21st century.

Second, the differences among teenagers, motor vehicles, professional athletes, the means of public transportation, magazines,
public schools, clergypersons, physicians, farms, and churches are
greater than ever before in American history. That helps to
explain why it is more difficult than ever before to produce a
good match between pastor and congregation.

Third, a growing body of research has redefined the problem.
Instead of bemoaning the shortage of talent, the new focus is on
the institutional environment. Does that institutional environment create a context for the placement of personnel and the
expectations projected of people that will lead to success or lead
to disaster? (See chapter 5.)

In 2002 it became clear that the institutional environment at
Arthur Andersen, the auditing partnership, had been transformed. For decades that institutional environment had placed
accuracy and integrity at the top of the value system. Those values also had attracted talented accountants and auditors. During
the 1990s an increase in profits had become the number-one
goal. That change in the institutional environment produced disaster for employees, investors, and retirees.

A second example was the Enron Corporation. The new focus
on "good numbers" offset the gifts and skills of valued employees.
Again, innocent investors, retirees, and employees were among
the victims of that disaster.

Too often in American Protestantism talented ministers are
"set up to fail" by being invited to serve churches where their
gifts, skills, experience, personality, and other characteristics do
not match the needs and culture of that congregation at this
point in its history. Occasionally the result is an overdue change
in that congregation's culture and direction. Far more often, however, the results include a disillusioned and often bitter pastor,
unhappy parishioners, shrinking participation, and an increase in
the number of unintentional interim pastorates. What can be
done about it? For at least three or four decades, the standard
response has been in-service educational events for the clergy.
Concurrently, the number of serious mismatches in the ministerial placement process has continued to increase.

For at least 40 years the standard response among traffic engineers to overcrowded highways was to construct additional lanes for motor vehicles. Thanks to modern technology, a new response is to increase the use of relevant information. The Federal Highway Administration is now allocating huge sums of money to create "intelligent transportation systems." This enables an urban community to track, predict, and control the flow of traffic, and thus increase capacity. The old approach called for using concrete to increase capacity. The new system calls for using information to increase capacity.

The translation of that into an ecclesiastical context is that a crucial component of a denominational church-growth strategy should include (a) increasing the quality, relevance, and variety of information that is fed into the ministerial placement process, and (b) raising the level of competence of those engaged in that process (ministers, search committee members, and denominational staff) in the productive use of that information. In other words, make the top denominational priority the creation of good matches between pastors and congregations. Instead of lamenting the shortage of talent, focus on creating a ministerial placement system that is designed to place ministers and lay program staff in congregational environments in which they will bloom. Models of this approach to the assignment of talent can be found in an increasing number of health care systems, several major league baseball teams, a modest number of public school districts, a rapidly growing number of profit-driven corporations, and thousands of new ventures pioneering the creation of a new product or a new service for the American marketplace.

Among the outcomes are happier people, healthier institutions, longer tenure for employees, greater productivity, an increased capability to adapt and respond creatively to new demands from the constituency being served, and an increase in the size of that constituency. Instead of "setting people up to fail," this "sets people up to succeed."

Many members of small churches might respond, "We want a pastor who is a lifelong lover, not someone who comes here to learn how to be a success in ministry elsewhere." Others will ask skeptically, "We've never had a minister who stayed more than five years. Do you think this could change that pattern?" At least a few will inquire, "Will you help us understand how we transform our congregational culture and our institutional environment to make that happen here?"

2. The recently arrived chief executive of this regional judicatory that includes 350 congregations of various types and sizes had explained earlier to the search committee that was charged with recommending a successor, "If you decide I am the person you seek, you need to understand my view of this role. Immediately after graduating from seminary, I went out to serve as the pastor of a congregation founded in 1993. It is located in a small city. When I arrived, the population was about 2,700, and the church had averaged 97 at worship the previous year. We spent five happy years there. I learned how to do ministry. I led worship, I preached, I taught an adult Sunday school class, I buried the dead, I officiated at weddings, I baptized, I called in two hospitals every week, I visited the shut-ins, I recruited two volunteers to help me build a youth group; I was an administrator, a shepherd, a leader, an evangelist, a fund-raiser, and a counselor. I learned how to do everything a minister can and should do."

"What was the outcome?" inquired a member of the search committee.

"When we left after five years, we were averaging 122 at worship. We had renovated the fellowship hall and the kitchen in that old building, we had doubled the size of the parking lot, we had received 79 new members over those five years, and we left the church with a balance of over $8,000 in the treasury. They had been running a deficit before we came," recalled this 53-year-old minister.

"Our second stop was at Trinity Church where I had been invited to join the staff as the minister of assimilation. As you know, it is one of the largest congregations in our denomination. I preached at the Saturday evening services and occasionally on Sunday mornings. My two primary responsibilities, however, were the assimilation of new members and the overall care of our network of lay volunteers. I had to change from being a generalist to learn two new specialties. After five years I was invited to replace the senior associate pastor, who had resigned to become the senior minister of one of our big churches in Oklahoma. After four years in that position, my colleague and mentor, the senior minister, declared I was ready to leave and become the senior minister of this church. In those nine years at Trinity and my 15 years here, I have learned the difference between doing ministry and making sure ministry happens."

"What do you mean by that?" interrupted another member of the search committee.

"During these past 29 years, I've been involved as a volunteer in three different regional judicatories, plus watching what happened with my counterparts in other denominations. My conclusion is both the staff and volunteer officials feel compelled to do ministry. That's what I felt compelled to do in my first pastorate. As I told you, I did everything. For the past 24 years, however, I have been in settings where my primary responsibility is to make sure ministry happens. That means depending on lots of others to do ministry, not trying to do everything myself. For example, I now make fewer hospital calls in a year than I made in a month in that first pastorate," explained this veteran pastor.

"If you choose me to be your next executive, that's the perspective I will bring to the position. I have limited knowledge of your operation, but with 350 congregations, I would hope that within a few years at least seven or eight will have accepted the role of serving as a teaching church to help others discover how to do ministry in the 21st century."

"Tell us more by what you mean when you refer to a teaching church," urged another member of the committee.

"Well, I'm hesitant to do that since at this time I don't know your assets or your needs," came the ready reply. "At least one, however, should specialize in how to help people in other congregations understand the role and power of music in proclaiming the gospel of Jesus Christ to younger generations. I do know you have one congregation that could model how to pull off a successful relocation of the meeting place. I believe you have at least two that model the multisite approach to ministry. I hope you have at least a couple that are able and willing to work with leaders in some of those 200-plus small churches who could affiliate with a mentor church but don't want to abandon their sacred meeting place. Since the data you provided me reports one-third of your 350 congregations averaged fewer than 58 at worship last year, I also would like to enlist at least a dozen larger congregations to enlist, equip, and support teams of volunteers to fill the ministerial role in some of the very small churches here."

Do or Facilitate?

This raises what may be the key question for regional denominational judicatories in American Protestantism in the 21st century. This can be illustrated by looking at six points on an eight-point spectrum. We will leave open the middle two points for the readers to fill in with other potential scenarios. At the far end of the spectrum are the regional judicatories that already are regarded by congregational leaders, especially those in the very large churches, as an irrelevant and obsolete institutional legacy created by deeply committed Christians, all of whom have been dead for decades.

Next to that point on this spectrum are those who believe the primary responsibility of congregations is to provide the money, volunteers, and energy required to achieve denominationally generated goals.

Next to that position are those who believe denominational agencies exist to do what individual congregations are unable to do. That long list includes the examination of candidates for ordination; the ordination of new additions to the clergy roster (a key responsibility in 1890 to enable that new minister to get a pass to ride on the railroad); enlisting, training, placing, supporting, and supervising missionaries to foreign countries; the production and distribution of resources for use by congregational leaders and teachers; organizing and operating a pension system for ministers; planting new missions; collecting and redistributing money; assisting congregations in searching for a new pastor; scheduling and hosting meetings; organizing and helping fund a variety of church-related institutions; creating, producing, and distributing a new hymnal; providing a Christian witness and a prophetic voice for that denomination on social, political, economic, and religious issues of the day; publishing and distributing a denominational magazine to reinforce denominational loyalty and unity; designing and hosting continuing education events for both the laity and the clergy; proclaiming the Christian gospel by way of radio as part of a national (or regional) presence for this denomination; and helping congregations celebrate their past when that day comes to disband.

While that is far from a complete list, it does illustrate two points. First, it describes the third point on this spectrum. Second, with the partial exception of the last responsibility on that list, today scores of megachurches are now doing what denominational agencies did in 1955.

We leave the next two points on his spectrum to be filled in by the reader's experiences and hopes, and move on to sixth. It represents a growing phenomenon that consists of two constituencies. The smaller of the two includes those who are dismayed by the increase in the degree of freedom in the American culture since 1960. This is reflected in dress codes, political parties, immigration, threats to the environment, educational institutions, retail trade, the allocation of tax dollars for public education, the behavior of retirees, meals, housing, reckless drivers, the increase in the number of home schoolers, magazines, newspapers, marriage, language, television, the workplace, and even in the churches. Americans are less inhibited, less driven by tradition, and more likely to believe they are free to make the decisions that will shape their future.

One response is the demand for more regulation. One expression of this is to expand the role of denominational agencies as regulatory bodies.[3] Among the contemporary examples are the Roman Catholic Church in America, the Southern Baptist Convention, The United Methodist Church, and the Episcopal Church in the United States.

From this observer's perspective, however, it appears the number of American adults who are eager to serve as regulators greatly exceeds the number who want to be regulated. That sentence helps to explain the large number of teenagers who drop out of high school, the growth of cable television, and the increase in the number of nondenominational megachurches.

The seventh point on this spectrum is filled by those who are completely satisfied with the current role, responsibilities, priorities, and allocation of resources in their local regional judicatory. That contentment more than offsets any dissatisfactions they may feel about the role and priorities of the national agencies of their denomination.

At the opposite end of this spectrum from where we began is the eighth point. This is the home of those who combine three convictions. First, the number-one priority for all denominational agencies is to help congregations fulfill the Great Commission.[4] Second, the most effective way to do this is to build on strength, not focus on weakness or problems. Third, that means challenging congregations with discretionary resources, a vision of the future, and a number of committed Christians among the laity who are waiting to be challenged and equipped to do ministry to fulfill their potential.

This is the place on this eight-point spectrum where the new regional executive described earlier is determined to enlist partners in doing ministry rather than expect that regional judicatory to do it. This also is the place on that spectrum where this author expects to find an audience for this book.

CHAPTER SEVENTEEN

WHAT WILL
TOMORROW BRING?

What will the ecclesiastical scene for American Protestantism look like in the year 2035? The safe answer is, only God knows. All that sinful human beings can do is to speculate. One base line for speculation is to look at what has been happening in recent years and make projections into the future based on contemporary trends.

What Is Your Reference Point?

One trend is illustrated by the Church of the Brethren, the Seventh-day Adventist Church, The United Methodist Church, and other traditions that include a large proportion of small congregations averaging fewer than 50 at worship.

An opposite trend is illustrated by the Southern Baptist Convention, the Presbyterian Church in America, the Baptist General Conference, the Evangelical Free Church in America, and scores of relatively new independent Protestant congregations. That has been to increase the number of very large con-gregations averaging more than a thousand at worship.

A third trend is illustrated by tens of thousands of white, largely suburban, and well-educated Christians who have decided their religious needs will be fulfilled by participation in a rela-tively small house church, usually consisting of five to 15 house-holds.

A fourth trend is sometimes described as "the shrinking mid-dle." This reflects the recent sharp increase in the number of very large congregations, the increase in the number of small churches, and the shrinking proportion that average between 100 and 800 at worship. A few observers go so far as to predict those American Protestant congregations currently averaging between 40 and 800 at worship should be placed on the list of endangered species.

The reader is encouraged to add one or two more trends based on the size of congregations and choose the one that will turn out to be the forerunner of tomorrow.

A completely different reference point begins by looking at what has been happening in the growth of Christianity in the Southern Hemisphere of this planet and use that in predicting what the future will bring to Christianity in North America.[1]

Another reference point is to look at the changes in the American culture that influence the institutional expression of the Christian faith in America. These changes include the impact of the privately owned motor vehicle; easily available and low-cost electricity; radio; television; affluence; and the geo-graphical separation of the place of residence from the place of work, the place of education, the place of retail trade, the place of recreation, the place of entertainment, and the place of wor-ship. That list also includes the growth of consumerism, individ-ualism, and the demand for meaningful choices. (See chapter 4 for an elaboration of this paragraph.) This is one of the most influential reference points for this book.

An overlapping reference point for predicting the future is the growing demand for community. The erosion of neighborhood ties, the Americanization of the descendents of immigrants to the

United States, the erosion of the influence of kinship ties, a growing number of bicultural marriages, the migratory nature of the American people, and the search for meaning in life replacing the old focus on survival goals have combined to create an unprecedented search for community. This observer is convinced that is the number-one reason to be optimistic about the future of congregations averaging 15 to 50 at worship. An even stronger reason for this optimism can be found in the history of Christianity.[2]

An overlapping reason for optimism is the demand for certainty. Back in 1987 a 40-year-old physician was diagnosed with a rare form of leukemia. Three years later he was cured. A decade later, in reflecting on his experience as an impatient recipient of care, he refers to the differences between "probably" and "certainty." As a physician, he was comfortable explaining to patients the probable outcome of a prescribed therapy. As a patient, he demanded certainty.[3]

That is not a new insight. For many centuries human beings have turned to religion in their search for certainty. Thomas may be the most frequently cited example in Christianity. That also explains the search of pulpit nominating committees for one-armed preachers. They are not interested in sermons that explain, "On the one hand, but on the other hand" in proclaiming the gospel of Jesus Christ. Ambiguity may be acceptable in picking a place to live, but most adults prefer certainty in their religious pilgrimage.

The translation of that is the small congregation that is a meaningful and cohesive community of believers and proclaims an unambiguous statement of the Christian faith is meeting two important needs. By contrast, irrelevance on both points is the road to oblivion, regardless of size.

Three Clouds on the Horizon

The pessimists usually turn to a different set of reference points in their efforts to identify what the future will bring. They deserve to be heard. The most widely discussed black cloud hovering over most small churches is the rising cost of compensation in the ministerial marketplace. As was explained in chapter 6, the financial cost of attracting and retaining the services of a seminary-educated and full-time resident pastor can become a problem.

One place where the sun is shining brightly is over many of those small churches in which the traditional pastoral responsibilities are now carried by committed and equipped laypersons. One of the most significant and very large examples of this trend consists of that growing number of Roman Catholic parishes in America that are not served by a resident priest. While a shortage of priests rather than money is the motivating factor, most of these parishioners are happy with the new arrangement. One reason may be their resident pastor is a woman, not a man. The Roman Catholic Church in America pioneered the concept of Saturday worship. More recently, Roman Catholics have been modeling the acceptance of women in the parish ministry.

A second cloud is the cost of maintaining a traditional meeting place. The house churches, of course, have eliminated this expense. For hundreds of thousands of American Christians, however, life is not complete without a set-apart sacred place to gather for the corporate worship of God and other events and activities. The importance of place to human beings may be one of the most neglected factors in church planning.[4] The most common solution has been to rely on the contributions of work and money by previous generations to provide the capital for that sacred place. Another is to depend on income from an endowment fund to maintain that inheritance. "Let the people who build it pay to maintain it" is the rationale.

The growing response, however, is the possibility of "having our cake and eating it too." That small worshiping community continues to meet in that same sacred place as the north campus of a large multisite church. This arrangement allows that small worshiping community to enjoy intimacy and avoid complexity and anonymity while having open access to the full range of ministries and opportunities provided by that full-service church, including top-quality and relevant preaching. (See chapter 6.)

The largest and darkest cloud is called competition. The competition among Christian congregations in America for potential future constituents is increasing every year. The privately owned motor vehicle, and the rising level of expectations younger generations bring to church are two of the most powerful forces behind this competition. The six most critical points of competition are (a) a precisely defined identification of the constituency that congregation (or denomination) is seeking to reach and serve; (b) an accurate perception of the needs that must be addressed to reach and serve that constituency; (c) ministries that offer a relevant and high-quality response to those needs; (d) a clear, unambiguous, internally consistent, and persuasive proclamation of "This is what we believe and what we teach"; (e) for a majority of the churches to be competitive, a convenient, accessible, and safe place to park a motor vehicle; and (f) a variety of opportunities for newcomers to gain a sense of belonging. For some the music affirms "this is where I belong." For many it is the teaching. For perhaps one-third it is the relevance and openness of the group life of that larger community. For at least one out of six new constituents it is a relevant challenge to use one's gifts and skills in doing ministry. For at least a few it is the satisfaction of "Finally I've found a place where I am being heard."

Denominational Alternatives

From a denominational perspective the competition to reach and serve younger generations and recent immigrants has produced a range of responses. One has been to sharply increase the number of new missions planted each year. Perhaps the most productive has been to double or triple the number of very large congregations. A third has been to encourage the multisite model described in chapters 6 and 7. A fourth has been to place a higher value on the impact of excellent preaching as defined in a culture filled with a search for certainty, with the power of projected visual imagery, and with a huge variety of exceptionally persuasive messages from skilled and attractive advocates of ideas, services, and goods. A fifth response has been to focus on restructuring that denominational system. A sixth has been to promote ecumenism. A seventh has been to withdraw from the arenas of high competition for future constituents such as the central cities and growing suburban communities. An eighth has been to focus on putting together a package of operational policies designed to increase the proportion of congregations in that denominational family that average fewer than 100 at worship. A ninth has been to concentrate on taking better care of the clergy in terms of compensation, pensions, health insurance, housing, and opportunities for new careers. A tenth, and for some the most attractive, has been to create an agenda that will support an expansion of intradenominational quarreling.

Which of these alternatives have been chosen by your denomination? How will that influence the future of your congregation?

One Other Scenario

From this observer's perspective a new version of the institutional expression of the Christian faith in America may turn out to be the dominant player on the American ecclesiastical scene in 2035. Will it be the megachurch with a huge staff, a big budget, an extensive seven-day-a-week ministry that owns an 80- to 300-acre site that provides convenient and safe parking for a couple thousand motor vehicles? Or, will it be the small worshiping community that averages 35, more or less, at worship, and is treasured for its intimacy, caring, spontaneity, mutual support, and warmth?

My prediction is, "Yes, both."

This model already exists. It includes one very large central meeting place; a large cadre of deeply committed lay volunteers who staff a variety of ministries on this central campus and at several dozen other sites; a long-tenured and creative minister of missions; a big package of traditional and nontraditional ministries, programs, and activities; and an internally clear and consistent message of "This is what we believe, what we teach, and what we do."

Those off-campus sites of 2035 typically will include dozens of relatively homogeneous small worshiping communities, perhaps several lay-led house churches; at least a couple of more traditional congregations averaging over 300 at worship that meet in buildings within 50 miles of that central campus; a substantial number of small congregations founded before 1970 that have petitioned to become a part of this ministry; at least four or five sister churches on other continents led by indigenous pastors and one or more ministries housed in large apartment buildings. These are in addition to the thousands of people who worship every week at that central campus.

Three Questions

If this model does turn out to be a large part of the American ecclesiastical scene in the 21st century, it will raise three questions for the leaders of small churches:

1. Do we want to help initiate and build that new model?
2. Or, do we prefer to wait until someone comes along and invites us to join a working model of this concept?
3. Or, do we conclude this is simply one more evidence that the devil is alive and at work in this world?

Will tomorrow bring a sky filled with black clouds? Or, will tomorrow be a bright and sunny day for small churches? That can turn out to be a self-fulfilling prophecy.

DISTRIBUTION OF CONGREGATIONS BY AVERAGE WORSHIP ATTENDANCE

	Assemblies of God	Baptist General Conference	Disciples of Christ	Episcopal Church	Evangelical Free Church
Year	2000	1999	2001	2000	2000
Congregations Reporting	7,210	889	2,627	7,347	1,342
Congregations not reporting	4,845	24	1,100+	48	204
Average Worship Attendance:					
3-9	130	2	31	183	3
10	74	0	19	71	0
11-14	211	5	43	204	1
15	117	3	35	52	1
16	54	1	10	56	1
17	48	1	5	57	0
18	84	0	17	50	1
19	38	0	10	50	1
20	238	6	45	65	2
21-24	287	7	67	237	0
25	254	37	45	72	15
26-29	247	7	56	225	6

Appendix A

	Assemblies of God	Baptist General Conference	Disciples of Christ	Episcopal Church	Evangelical Free Church
Year	2000	1999	2001	2000	2000
Congregations Reporting	7,210	889	2,627	7,347	1,342
Congregations not reporting	4,845	24	1,100+	48	204
Average Worship Attendance:					
30	333	12	57	74	17
31-34	223	14	49	207	5
35	299	12	59	65	13
36-39	235	19	60	65	14
40	380	5	43	204	1
41-45	453	29	92	234	19
46-50	627	29	124	266	46
51-60	1,009	56	188	459	73
61-70	732	40	209	392	56
71-100	1,828	132	467	1,037	179
101-125	770	82	258	652	95
126-200	1,495	213	391	1,199	225
201-500	1,305	173	220	1,079	244
501+	468	61	25	148	111

Appendix A

	Evangelical Lutheran Church in America	Presbyterian Church in America	Presbyterian Church (U.S.A.)	Southern Baptist Convention	United Methodist Church
Year	2001	2001	2001	2000	1999
Congregations Reporting	10,764	1,187	9,460	35,616	38,874
Congregations not reporting	?	49	1,683	?	735
Average Worship Attendance:					
3-9	39	11	141	275	945
10	29	5	80	181	508
11-14	67	10	185	451	1,207
15	56	6	122	326	644
16	29	4	52	132	168
17	32	0	37	124	304
18	46	4	85	222	508
19	21	1	36	92	212
20	91	12	205	576	802
21-24	108	10	248	621	1,245
25	104	14	204	680	837
26-29	161	8	166	649	1,192
30	122	28	237	851	896
31-34	175	14	156	598	1,044
35	133	26	233	791	842
36-39	198	12	160	631	1,006
40	144	27	269	1,004	782
41-45	342	39	382	1,405	1,579
46-50	370	50	273	1,663	1,444
51-60	669	80	602	2,529	2,483
61-70	681	67	604	2,264	2,093
71-100	1,689	213	1,301	5,619	4,298
101-125	1,115	99	738	2,726	2,134
126-200	2,047	195	1,343	5,217	3,628
201-500	1,023	197	1,231	4,526	3,302
501+	?????	69	266	1,433	727

MEDIAN SIZE OF CONGREGATIONS AS MEASURED BY AVERAGE WORSHIP ATTENDANCE

Assemblies of God	97
Baptist General Conference	110
Church of the Brethren	58
Church of the Nazarene	66
Christian Church (Disciples of Christ)	71
Episcopal Church U.S.A.	79
Evangelical Covenant Church	98
Evangelical Free Church in America	135
Evangelical Lutheran Church in America	100
Free Methodist Church	56
Lutheran Church-Missouri Synod	125
Presbyterian Church in America	98
Presbyterian Church (U.S.A.)	74
Reformed Church in America	112
Southern Baptist Convention	70
United Church of Christ	74
United Methodist Church	53
Wesleyan Church	59
Wisconsin Evangelical Lutheran Synod	93

NOTES

Introduction

1. This is the central theme of Lyle E. Schaller, *From Geography to Affinity: How Congregations Can Learn from One Another* (Nashville: Abingdon Press, 2003).

2. Alternative sources of income for denominational systems are identified in Lyle E. Schaller, *The New Context for Ministry: Competing for the Charitable Dollar* (Nashville: Abingdon Press, 2002), 273-312.

1. How Do You Define Small?

1. United States Bureau of the Census, *Religious Bodies 1906* (Washington, D.C.: Government Printing Office, 1910).

2. Dale E. Jones, et al. *Religious Congregational Membership in the United States 2000* (Nashville: Glenmary Research Center, 2002).

3. A useful review of the role of house churches as an expression of religious dissent in 17th- and 18th-century Europe is the essay by Benjamin J. Kaplan, "Fictions of Privacy: House Chapels in the Spatial Accommodations of Religious Dissent in Early Modern Europe," *American Historical Review*, vol. 107, no. 4 (October 2002): 1031-64.

4. One resource for these very large congregations is *The Large Church Letter* by Lyle E. Schaller and Herb Miller. For information contact Herb Miller, 3805 94th Place, Lubbock, TX 79423-3913, or email HrbMiller@aol.com. Another is Lyle E. Schaller, *The Very Large Church* (Nashville: Abingdon Press, 2000).

2. That's Not a Category!

1. Lee S. Shulman, "Making Differences: A Table of Learning," *Change* (November/December 2002): 37.

3. Why So Many?

1. Countless books have been written on the role of small groups in the church. The pioneering research on how the physical environment influences human behav-

ior is Roger G. Barker, *Ecological Psychology* (Stanford: Stanford University Press, 1968). Those interested in building groups around high commitment and sacrifice on the behalf of others may profit from Thomas E. Ricks, *Making the Corps* (New York: Scribner, 1997). Those seeking a more sophisticated explanation of why people behave as they do, using mathematical game theory, may want to begin with a pioneering book in that field, Otomar J. Bartos, *Simple Models of Group Behavior* (New York: Columbia University Press, 1967). This observer's early reflections are summarized in the chapter "Small Groups and Large Groups" in Lyle E. Schaller, *Effective Church Planning* (Nashville: Abingdon Press, 1979), 17-63. An exceptionally good book that is a case study of how to build a high-commitment congregation is Michael Slaughter, *The Learning Church* (Loveland, Colo.: Group Publishing, 2002).

4. The 21st-century Context

1. An introduction to this research can be found in Marvin Lazerson, Ursula Wagener, and Nichole Shumann, "Teaching and Learning in Higher Education, 1980–2000," *Change* (May/June 2000): 13-19.
2. Will Herberg, *Protestant, Catholic, Jew* (Garden City, New York: Doubleday & Co., 1955).
3. This line or demarcation is described in Lyle E. Schaller, *What Have We Learned?* (Nashville: Abingdon Press, 2001), 63-78.
4. The pioneering book on this subject is Aaron Wildavsky, *The Rise of Radical Egalitarianism* (Washington, D.C.: The American University Press, 1991).
5. This is the theme of Lyle E. Schaller, *The New Context for Ministry: Competing for the Charitable Dollar* (Nashville: Abingdon Press, 2002). See especially pages 177-271.
6. A useful brief introduction to this development is Philip Jenkins, "The Next Christianity," *The Atlantic* (October 2002): 53-68.

5. Superstar or Talented Team?

1. David Nevin, *Left-Handed Fastballers: Scouting and Training America's Grass-Roots Leaders, 1966–1977* (New York: The Ford Foundation, 1981).
2. An excellent brief introduction to this debate is Malcolm Gladwell, "The Talent Myth," *The New Yorker* (July 22, 2002): 28-33.
3. The cover story on *Christianity Today* (November 18, 2002).
4. A. G. Pritchard, *Willow Creek Seeker Services* (Grand Rapids, Mich.: Baker Books, 1996), 11-48, 124-36.
5. Howard Edington, *Downtown Church: The Heart of the City* (Nashville: Abingdon Press, 1996).
6. Claude E. Payne and Hamilton Beasley, *Reclaiming the Great Commission* (San Francisco: Jossey-Bass, 2000).
7. B. Carlisle Driggers, *A Journey of Faith and Hope* (Columbia, S.C.: The R. L. Bryan Company, 2000).

8. This concept of a team of teams in the very large churches is discussed in Lyle E. Schaller, *Discontinuity and Hope* (Nashville: Abingdon Press, 1999), 109-14.

6. Empower the Laity!

1. About a dozen years ago I borrowed the term "free agent" from major league baseball to identify the early retirement laypersons who were bringing a high level of skill, relevant experiences, commitment, and creativity to the program staff of very large congregations. It also has been used in discussions of a recent trend in the secular labor force. A key concept in understanding what motivates these free agents has been contributed by Bob Buford, *Half-Time* (Grand Rapids, Mich.: Zondervan Publishing House, 1994). Buford describes this as the transition "from success to significance." It should be noted that Buford did not wait to be challenged. He took the initiative. That helps to explain why many of the most gifted and entrepreneurial free agents prefer to pioneer the new rather than attempt to perpetuate or reform the old.

2. An excellent experience-based statement on the value of indigenous leadership is J. Timothy Ahlen and J. V. Thomas, *One Church, Many Congregations* (Nashville: Abingdon Press, 1999), 77-90.

3. Lyle E. Schaller, *Innovations in Ministry* (Nashville: Abingdon Press, 1994), 64-85.

7. The Affiliate Relationship

1. This new era is described in an experience-based book by Rob Weber, *Visual Leadership: The Church Leader as ImageSmith* (Nashville: Abingdon Press, 2002).

2. For an introduction to this shift in the focus of higher education from teaching to learning see *Change: The Magazine of Higher Learning* (November/December 2001). For a review of the impact of the Fund for the Improvement of Postsecondary Education (FIPSE), see *Change* (September/October 2002).

3. The healing of the wounded bird is discussed in greater detail in Lyle E. Schaller, *Innovations in Ministry* (Nashville: Abingdon Press, 1994), 98-111.

10. The Endowed Church

1. This issue is discussed in greater detail in Lyle E. Schaller, *The New Context for Ministry: Competing for the Charitable Dollar* (Nashville: Abingdon Press, 2002).

Notes

11. Is Numerical Growth a Goal?

1. For a description of this role, see Lyle E. Schaller, *The Interventionist* (Nashville: Abingdon Press, 1997).

2. A provocative statement on the criteria to be used in evaluating a contemporary religious movement is Douglas Rushkoff, "Don't Judge Judaism by the Numbers," *New York Times*, November 20, 2002, A-31. The letters to the editors (p. 2) days later help to explain why this is a divisive issue.

12. What About Those Ninth-graders?

1. This type and size congregation is the subject of an earlier book, Lyle E. Schaller, *The Middle Sized Church* (Nashville: Abingdon Press, 1985).

13. Should We Merge?

1. For a more detailed discussion of this distinction between mergers and unions, see Lyle E. Schaller, *Mergers and Unions of Local Churches*, a monograph (Naperville, Ill.: The Center for Parish Development, 1969).

14. Three Technological Scenarios

1. Kathleen Hall Jamieson, *Eloquence in an Electronic* Age (New York: Oxford University Press, 1986).

16. A Denominational Perspective

1. For a discussion of this denominational priority, see Lyle E. Schaller, *What Have We Learned?* (Nashville: Abingdon Press, 2001), 197-213.

2. This priority may be the most effective strategy for the transformation of lives. See Schaller, *What Have We Learned?* 119-23.

3. The pioneering discussion on the role of American Protestant denominations as regulatory bodies is Craig Dystra and James Hudnut-Beumler, "The National Organizational Structures of Protestant Denominations," Milton J. Coalter, et al., eds., *The Organizational Revolution* (Louisville: Westminster/John Knox Press, 1992), 307-31.

4. See Payne and Beasley, *Reclaiming the Great Commission*, and Driggers, A *Journey of Faith and Hope*.

17. What Will Tomorrow Bring?

1. Philip Jenkins, "The Next Christianity," *The Atlantic Monthly* (October 2002): 53-68. For another perspective, see the interview with Donald Miller by Timothy Sato in *Books & Culture* (November/December 2002): 31-35.

2. Among the thousands of book and articles on Christianity and community, several dozens stand out. One is Robert Banks, *Paul's Idea of Community: The Early House Churches in Their Historical Setting* (Grand Rapids, Mich.: Wm. B. Eerdmans Publishing Company, 1988).

3. Geoffrey Kurland, *My Own Medicine* (New York: Times Books/Henry Holt & Company, 2002).

4. For an elaboration of this point, see Lyle E. Schaller, *Effective Church Planning* (Nashville: Abingdon Press, 1979), 65-92.